THE KEYS TO OUR SUCCESS

2nd Edition

LESSONS LEARNED FROM 29 OF OUR BEST PROJECT MANAGERS

Compiled by

David Barrett & Kathi Soniat

Published by

KEBS Publishing, Collingwood, Ontario

The Keys to Our Success – 2nd Edition
Lessons Learned from 29 of our Best Project Managers

Compiled by David Barrett & Kathi Soniat

Editor: Melanie Vollick

Published by:
KEBS Publishing
Collingwood, Ontario

Production © 2019 by KEBS Publishing
ISBN-9781709936289

*For all the project managers with whom
I have walked over these years.*

David

*To my husband James, who has given his support
through multiple careers. Providing patience and
guidance along each path of the journey.*

Kathi

TABLE OF CONTENTS

LIST OF AUTHORS

FORWARD

The best way to learn is from experience and in the project management business that can be difficult. We don't all have the opportunity to see and experience different scenarios and environments that would make us better project managers. But others have and they typically have a lot of stories to tell and experiences to share that can help us all.

This is the second edition of The Keys to Our Success. The first was published in 2013 by David Barrett and Derek Vigar. It was a great success and enjoyed by many.

Now, almost seven years later, it seemed time to do it again.

Kathi Soniat and David Barrett have teamed up to produce another collection of lessons learned from some of our best project managers.

We went out to all the project managers we know and offered them a chance to be a part of this new book. The ask was simple: if you had to boil your project management success down to just one tool, technique, idea or nugget, what would it be?

This book is a collection of their best lessons learned. It contains the kind of insights you would seek from the most trusted of mentors. Each chapter gives a different project leader a chance to share his or her key to success. Their stories, examples, and takeaways are invaluable, especially if you are someone looking for "what's really important"

We hope you enjoy this second edition of the Keys to Our Success.

Kathi and David

DAVID BARRETT

is a professional speaker, regular blogger, podcast host, author/compiler of 7 books and education advisor. His career includes the creation and directing of a project management conference business: ProjectWorld and Project Summit, a training company, a software development firm, a speaker bureau, a project management portal called ProjectTimes.com and a TED-style event series for project professionals across North America.

David Barrett can be reached at dbarrett@solutionsnetwork.com

KATHI SONIAT

is a PMP certified project manager and avid reader/reviewer. Highlights include: member of the release team for Liz Wiseman's Rookie Smarts, a beta "listener" of Dan Pink's podcast and beta reader for Elizabeth Harrin's book Overcoming Impostor Syndrome. She has served on the board of the PMI Palmetto Chapter as President and Past President.

Kathi Soniat can be reached at ksoniat77@gmail.com

CREATING VALUE - THE ONLY REASON TO DO A PROJECT

DAN WATT

WHY DO PROJECTS?

It is not to create new technology solutions or to create new marketing programs or to outsource a function or build a building or any of the myriad of things that projects build. It is to generate value in the **easiest and least expensive** manner possible. Not just generate value, but in the easiest, least expensive manner. If there are multiple ways to generate the same value, why would we choose a harder, more expensive way?

The things we build are to provide an outcome that can be turned into what we or your client value. This is called a value chain and every project should have one.

In 2019, we celebrated the 50th anniversary of the moon landing, and I'm barely old enough to remember watching the Apollo missions as a kid. In 1963, JF Kennedy said, "We will go to the moon by the end of the decade." It was the height of the cold war and he went on to explain that achieving this goal would demonstrate the technical prowess of the US over Russia, allowing the US to help ensure the new technology would be used for good and not ill.

There were three options that were considered; it was the moon landing that the US felt it had a chance of winning over Russia, it was also **the most difficult and most expensive.** It was forecasted to cost $22B and came in at $25.4B (around $150B today) and it was a significant portion of the US budget at the time.

Hold on! The purpose of a project is to create value in the easiest, least expensive manner. Why did they choose the most difficult, most expensive option? The short answer is: risk. The other two options that were considered were to put a lab into orbit around the Earth or send a man to orbit around the moon and return to Earth. Both those options were less expensive and easier; but, it was felt that Russia would beat the US to those goals. Therefore, those projects were riskier. If Russia completed them first, the US would not be able to demonstrate their technology dominance and therefore the project would not create the desired outcome (value). Going to the moon was the easiest, least expensive option and while it was a risky project, in fact, people could die. It was the least risky option of the three to get the desired outcome. Note: they did not choose to go to Mars which would have been significantly more complex and more expensive.

VALUE CREATION

Value or outcome is measured by what a project produces. Outcome should be frequently measurable and directly attributable to the project. Being on time and on budget are important but by themselves do not usually create value; many successful projects go over budget and take longer than anticipated at the start.

By all measures the US space program was successful. The amount of innovation that came out of the program demonstrated US technology dominance and propelled the US economy forward for decades after the program was over. Russia was not able to exceed or even match the accomplishment.

The moon landing is an example of a well-crafted goal. It has a clearly measurable end point (land a man on the moon and safely return him) and a timeline for getting there (end of the decade). It also has a defined value chain – that is, things that the project itself will not deliver but will enable - the US technology dominance over Russia so that it could control space.

How many of the projects that you work on have clearly defined outcomes with a timeline and a value chain that shows the effects the project will have on a larger scale? Can the sponsors of the project articulate the value? In my experience, most project teams are trying to get the product (whatever it is) built within a budget and timeframe. Whether it does what was intended is rarely a success criterion. I have seen technology projects almost cripple businesses when they go live. The sponsor is just as much to blame as the project team because as the sponsor often chooses the solution for the team and says "implement this." They do not articulate desired outcomes and let the team find the most suitable solution for the problem. Then, wonder why the solution does not do what they wanted when it is finished.

VALUE CHAIN

What is a value chain and why is important?

Most business cases promise to deliver some sort of financial value: increased sales, decreased costs, and so on. However, most projects and project teams do not have responsibility to make sure those things are delivered. In the Apollo mission the team was not responsible for showing technical prowess over Russia and all that came with that, their job was to land a man on the moon and safely bring him back.

Let's say you are working on a technology project to build some sort of new product or service. The project is going to cost $2 million and someone, usually finance or the CEO says, what's the ROI (Return on investment) – when do we get our money back on this investment?

This is a reasonable question to ask the sponsor of the project, it is not a reasonable question to ask the team responsible for building the solution. The team likely does not have responsibility for marketing, sales or any of the other functions that will bring dollars in the door. That is probably the sales executive or business leader.

So, what is the solution team responsible for? Good question! And, one that is often not answered or not well defined. When the solution does not hit the mark and the intended value is not created, the finger pointing starts. The business says, "The tech team didn't deliver what we needed," - the tech team says, "The business didn't tell us what they wanted" - sound familiar?

Would it not be better if there were clearly defined outcomes for each of the teams? And, those outcomes were frequently measurable and directly attributable to the work being done by the team.

In the example above, what if the project team's outcome was to build a product that would be used by 75% of the existing client base in the first six months or have 25,000 new people try the new service in the first three months with 10% of them signing up for the service. Those targets could be measured daily, and the product or service tweaked after the live date to address concerns in hitting the target. By the way, this is where the Agile methodology starts to shine – constant pivoting to address concerns based on facts.

VALUE CHAIN EXAMPLE

A new website is developed. Goal is to increase revenue by 20% and profitability by 25%. Each team has a part in the creation of revenue and profitability. The web development team is not responsible for revenue or profitability. In this case they are accountable for adoption.

HOW DOES VALUE PLAY INTO DAY TO DAY PROJECT MANAGEMENT?

Value or outcome is the basis for ALL decisions that are made in a project. Without value definitions for each project, decisions are based on the desires of the sponsor or others on the project. Without defined value for each project, the best resources may not be assigned to the projects creating the most value.

Frequently available data points allow decisions to be fact based. If those measures are widely available across the team everyone is on the same page when decisions are made, and the entire team pulls in the same direction.

PROJECT PORTFOLIO VALUE FRAMEWORK

If every project in a company's portfolio has clearly defined outcomes and value chains, it is much easier to show the overall value being created by the investments made in projects. The value can be categorized to show a balance in the types of investments the company is making.

Does your company know how much it invests in regulatory work, safety and soundness, new product development, and efficiencies? Do project sponsors and project managers know how to classify their projects so that a roll up can be done?

This approach is similar to the investments in your financial portfolio. You might say to your financial advisor, I would like a 6% annual return on my portfolio at a medium risk level. That does not mean they will not make some riskier investments as they have the potential for a large return. It means they will likely offset those investments with some low risk investments that will have a lower return.

You should think of your project portfolio like you think about your personal financial portfolio. Projects have an added complication; there are some projects that are strictly for safety and soundness or regulatory work and they do not have a return so the remaining projects will have to return more to compensate for these projects. What is your desired annual return on your project portfolio? I have talked with several executives about this concept and they do not don't know what return they want. They just want the projects to get done. Would you ever say to your financial advisor, "I don't know what return I want, just make some investments?" - Probably not. Project management offices need to drive this conversation. It is their value proposition.

Below is a sample structure for categorizing Value. It really does not matter what categories you use as long as there is consistency across all projects so the numbers can be rolled up.

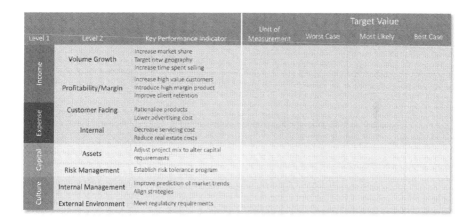

Level 1	Level 2	Key Performance Indicator	Unit of Measurement	Target Value		
				Worst Case	Most Likely	Best Case
Income	Volume Growth	Increase market share Target new geography Increase time spent selling				
	Profitability/Margin	Increase high value customers Introduce high margin product Improve client retention				
Expense	Customer Facing	Rationalize products Lower advertising cost				
	Internal	Decrease servicing cost Reduce real estate costs				
Capital	Assets	Adjust project mix to alter capital requirements				
	Risk Management	Establish risk tolerance program				
Culture	Internal Management	Improve prediction of market trends Align strategies				
	External Environment	Meet regulatory requirements				

CONCLUSION

When assigned a project, the most important question you must ask is: what value/outcome is my team responsible for generating? Then you can figure out options for delivering those outcomes. Too many times I see project teams doing it the other way around. Without a definition for project outcomes, how do decisions get made on your project?

If you run a project management office, rolling up the value of each project and working with the executives to set a portfolio target and ensuring that the target is met is the value you bring to the company.

DAN WATT

Over his career, Dan Watt has run large programs that generate business value through technology and process redesign. He has set up five project management offices across multiple geographies for large corporations having led teams in Canada, the US, Europe, Asia, and Australia.

Through his own software company, he has helped companies transform as they take advantage of technology that his company has built. His work has crossed many industries and it is that cross pollination of ideas that brings creativity to his projects. He is a firm believer in looking outside of industry for inspiration and solutions.

Projects and process design are not just for corporations. He sat on the board of a childhood cancer foundation where he was part of a team that organized a 19-day bicycle ride across Canada that raised over $1 million for childhood cancer. He sits on the board of his local cycling organization where he has implemented systems and processes to simplify the running of the club.

When not running projects, Dan spends his time renovating houses, traveling, cycling and engaging in his passion for photography.

Dan can be reached at dan.watt@outlook.com or on LinkedIn at: www.linkedin.com/in/danwatt

MINDFULNESS AND WISDOM FOR OPTIMAL PERFORMANCE

GEORGE PITAGORSKY

Two primary keys to success in project work are wisdom and mindfulness. They enable the blending of the critical success factors of healthy relationships and cognitive readiness to effectively manage in the face of volatility, uncertainty, complexity, and ambiguity. Healthy relationships and cognitive readiness promote responsiveness, effective conflict resolution and rational expectations, with everyone understanding what to expect and what is expected of them. Healthy relationships and cognitive readiness lead to the optimal performance of project planning and execution and to improving the probability of success.

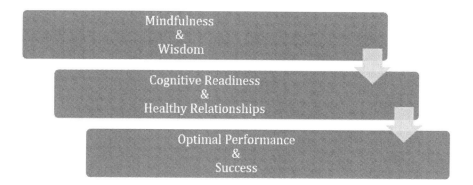

Figure 1: Keys to Success

PRACTICAL APPLICATION

A performance improvement program sought to change the work process in a highly regulated organization with over 8,000 employees, many in labor unions, across 1500 locations. The program was planned to be executed within five years. The organization had not experienced major organizational change in decades and was change resistant, even though everyone agreed that change was necessary. Success would be measured by the improved performance of the organization as perceived by its customers, executive management and key employees (particularly the managers of the individual locations and their staff).

Wisdom and mindfulness of the cause and effect relationships at play led to a system and process-based approach. Wisdom recognized the need to go beyond technology and process change to focus heavily on the human factors involved. It recognized the need to work with the interactions among program and project team members, business unit management, executives, regulators, vendors, employees, labor unions and customers in a complex system. Wisdom saw clearly that change and uncertainty were inevitable and that expectations needed to be managed through clear and regular communications.

Mindfulness of emotions like anxiety, frustration, and anger helped to manage the pressures associated with changing requirements. As well as and the coming and going of key stakeholders, schedule slippage, resistance to change, control issues between a program management office and business unit management, delays in deliverables from external groups who had little or no accountability, and politically motivated irrational demands from sponsors and clients.

SUCCESS

Success is satisfying stakeholder expectations. It is based on the ability to approach each project as a unique opportunity to perform optimally - sustainably achieving multiple - often competing - objectives as effectively as possible, given current real-world conditions.

Optimal performance requires striking the right dynamic balance between peak performance, high performance, and rest. It requires cognitive readiness and healthy relationships, and these require mindfulness and wisdom.

MINDFULNESS

Mindfulness is the ability to observe objectively and to be responsive as opposed to reactive. Jon Kabat-Zinn, a leading expert in mindfulness and originator of Mindfulness Based Stress Reduction (MBSR) describes mindfulness as "awareness that arises through paying attention, on purpose, in the present moment, non-judgmentally," and "in the service of self-understanding and wisdom."[1]

Everyone is mindful to some degree. That degree can be enhanced with formal and moment-to-moment mindfulness meditation practice until it becomes the natural way of perceiving one's world.

WISDOM

Across the many definitions of wisdom, it is widely accepted that wisdom goes beyond intellectual understanding. Wisdom is the transformation of experience, knowledge, common sense, insight and good judgement into understanding and effective action.

A recent study "found that participant levels of the character, strengths of wisdom,"[2] enhanced performance and reduced stress. The character strengths studied are fairness, compassion, love, curiosity, kindness and judgement.

Wisdom recognizes the interconnection among behavior, people and things, as in systems and process thinking. Everything is interconnected through causes and effects in a system made up of many subsystems. Everything is subject to change. The effects of change are not 100% predictable, especially in complex systems.

Wisdom is associated with self-knowledge, interconnectedness, and the reality that everything including one's mental states is caused by something: address the cause to change its effect.

The Serenity Prayer says wisdom is the ability to know the difference between the things one can change and the things that they cannot change. Wisdom recognizes that we have some control. But, while we can learn to surf, we cannot control the ocean.

Thanissaro Bhikku, an expert in Buddhist thought, says "For all the subtlety of his teachings, the Buddha had a simple test for measuring wisdom. 'You are wise', he said, to the extent that you can get yourself to do things you don't like doing but know will result in happiness, and to refrain from doing what you like but know will result in pain or harm."[3]

World religious and philosophical traditions view wisdom as central to the ability to live a successful and happy life. For project managers, success and happiness equate to delivering results to satisfy stakeholders.

Inuit wisdom translates nicely into wise guidelines for people working on projects - plan, hone your motivation, and your technical and relationship skills, so that you can work harmoniously to collaboratively achieve objectives that serve the organization and its ecosystem.[4]

WISDOM IMPLIES ETHICAL BEHAVIOR

Because we know that action without wisdom may cause harm, wisdom includes ethical behavior. The PMI Code of ethics reflects this by stating that PMs should:

- Take responsibility for the consequences of their decisions and actions
- Inform yourself and follow policies, rules, regulations and laws and report unethical or illegal conduct
- Respect yourself, respect others and their norms and customs, and respect the assets, reputation, environment and resources entrusted to the project and its stakeholders
- Be fair - impartial and objective - in decisions and actions
- Be honest and truthful

MINDFULNESS AND WISDOM

Mindfulness enhances wisdom by enabling insight and responsiveness through the clear, objective observation of things as they are. Wisdom leads to greater mindfulness by enabling the individual to let go of unfounded beliefs and to focus on what is real and critical to optimal performance.

Mindfulness and wisdom enable cognitive readiness and healthy relationships. These are critical, project management success factors.

COGNITIVE READINESS

Cognitive readiness (CR) is being ready for anything, dynamically balancing all of the leadership, technical and organizational factors required to succeed. As defined in the U. S. military, "Cognitive readiness is the mental preparation (including skills, knowledge, abilities, motivations, and personal dispositions) an individual needs to establish and sustain competent performance in the complex and unpredictable environment of modern ... operations." [3] https://apps.dtic.mil/dtic/tr/ fulltext/u2/a417618.pdf Success relies on being calm, cool and collected - ready for anything.

To be cognitively ready requires emotional and social intelligence - the ability to manage one's own emotional responses and to be aware of the emotional needs of others. It is this intelligence that enables one to be responsive and non-reactive without suppressing one's natural emotions. Mindfulness enables awareness of emotions as they arise and before they "take over." Wisdom knows it is alright to experience anger, fear, and other unpleasant emotions. It is how one relates to them and responds that matters.

HEALTHY RELATIONSHIPS

Projects are collaborative efforts. Healthy relationships result from mindful communication and the wisdom that harmony adds value. Healthy relationships are the foundation for making working together a pleasant and fulfilling experience which results in optimal outcomes. The keys to healthy relationships are managing conflicts and expectations wisely with mindful communication.

MANAGING CONFLICTS

Projects are filled with conflicts – some productive and some not. Productive conflicts are those over content issues such as design choices or priorities, which result in effective solutions. When managed well, conflict leads to greater harmony among team members who can exchange opposing views and criticism without being caught up in anger and defensiveness.

Destructive conflicts are those that become emotionally charged and personal. Mindfulness enables the emotional intelligence needed to avoid becoming identified with one's opinions and to catch the emotional charge that comes up when questioned or confronted with opposition. Wisdom reminds stakeholders of the importance of harmony and being open, objective, and impartial.

MANAGING EXPECTATIONS

Projects are successful when stakeholder expectations are met. Wisdom recognizes that irrational expectations get in the way of success. Irrational expectations are irrational because they cannot be met. Irrational demands include certainty, adding and changing requirements without impacting the schedule and budget and getting things done on time without sufficient resources. Mindfulness with emotional intelligence enables the courage to confront irrational demands and remind stakeholders of the uncertainty they wish was not a factor in their project.

KEYS TO SUCCESS

Cognitive readiness and healthy relationships are critical success factors enabled by mindfulness and wisdom.

- **Mindfulness** is the ability to purposefully observe everything that occurs in or around oneself objectively. It is the foundation for responsive as opposed to reactive behavior, enabling emotional and social intelligence and the ability to collaborate.

- **Wisdom** is realistically accepting things as they are - subject to change based on cause and effect relationships among people and their behavior. It recognizes the importance of harmony based on respect, ethical values, and truthfulness. It recognizes that volatility, uncertainty, complexity and ambiguity are facts of life that must be accepted and managed.

GEORGE PITAGORSKY

George Pitagorsky is a globally recognized project management thought leader. As a consultant, coach, speaker and facilitator, he works to improve performance by applying mindfulness meditation and systems as well as and process thinking.

George has a decade long career in project and program management as a practitioner, consultant and trainer. He has served as Chief Information Officer (CIO) for a multi-billion-dollar organization and co-founded Software Design Associates. As the Director of Product Development for an international learning organization, he developed methodologies, courses and curricula for major globally known clients.

He has authored three books that apply mindfulness in organizations, The Zen Approach to Project Management, Managing Conflict in Projects and Managing Expectations: A Mindful Approach to Achieving Optimal Performance. George recently authored *How to Be Happy Even When You Are Sad, Mad, or Scared*. He also produces the Breakthrough Newsletter.

Contact: www.PitagorskyConsulting.com
email: Info@PitagorskyConsulting.com

BE HUMBLE

JONATHAN CINELLI

I have thought a lot about what makes a successful project manager. It's a heavy statement and can be very subjective based on the external cultural environment, industry requirements, and personal perceptions.

Since many of our discussions in today's world tend to be resolved based on what Google says, it is rather easy to say that according to Google if you "accomplish an aim on purpose" you would be defined as "successful"

My thoughts are dramatically different than Google defines it as. I believe that the Google definition needs to be morphed together with the specific requirements of a project and the project manager.

I think of a project as anything with a set of expectations which - when met - is considered accomplished. The next part that is more alluring and intriguing to me - Manager, according to the Oxford dictionary is "to be responsible for controlling an organization, group of staff." To elaborate on this definition, if we control the people, reach the goals, the medal for becoming a successful project manager will be awarded to us.

I, however, have an issue with the use of the word "control," considering that every human being is the captain of their own vessel and entirely the commander of the decisions one makes. Attempting to highjack the neural-pathways of decision making and reworking a hard-wired system has a crisis looming. Simply ask any parent who has been around a young child who was fixated on something which was not given to them. It may have led to an emotional breakdown. The outcomes are no different with adults; the reactions and language may be expressed alternatively through a variety of actions, results and outputs.

Another fundamental word associated with the definition of a successful project manager is the term expert. Defined by "a person who has comprehensive and authoritative knowledge of or skill in a particular area," the term expert may be a ticking time bomb waiting to explode. An expert could be quite subjective based on the person expressing the view and the lens through which they are looking.

For instance, is a tennis pro with 15 years experience (who has played at a competitively high level their entire life, yet never won a championship) considered an expert? After all, they have comprehensive and authoritative knowledge of a skill and sport. Who is an expert? You decide.

We have now established what a successful project manager is using all the key words and validated them with formal definitions. It becomes apparent that the framework for a successful project manager may not be as 'clear as day'. In fact, it may be closer in resemblance to a bucket half full of murky swamp water. More modestly, a successful project manager is defined by a plethora of professionals using different parameters, variables, perspectives and analogies, which are chosen to be used as the measuring tool. This is no different than the discussions that would occur to define whether the tennis pro is, or is not, an expert.

We live in a history defining period where access to information and resources are at our fingertips. Our project managers are becoming stronger, better educated and more dynamic than ever before. The way in which we learn and communicate with one another has developed at such a rapid pace, that expectations for immediate action have become a standard operating procedure. Not being connected is now a page in the history books; instantaneous reactions are the new cultural norm.

This advancement comes at a cost which goes much deeper than its monetary value and most certainly affects the bottom line of our organizations, which include the people who embody them. The same conscious and unconscious energy which created the advancement can also lead to the collapse of great people, organizations, and mindsets. Packaged a little different for everyone, universal to all- one's ego has the divine power to infiltrate the minds of many and shifting realities. A person's ego is not always negative. When embraced openly, with awareness and operating from the proper mindset it can lead to rewarding outcomes. Our ego can help us to balance internal thoughts and filter them to the reality of the external world. Strong egos have helped to develop wonderful inventions and create world class human beings.

I invite our current and our future project managers to shift their realities and open their minds to a new realm of what could possibly be, in the world of project management. I am going to connect this to the construction sector, a reality of my existence. Traditionally, this is a sector where profit margins have been measured more by the quantity of widgets, bricks and mortar, than emotional intelligence and personal assets. Competing fixed mindsets and egos constantly visit the construction space. At times, they stay for a short period; but, many times an ego will over extend its stay.

My experiences led me to one guiding principle which has been my compass along this journey. This tool can turn even the most complex construction projects with challenging teams into a pleasure and honour to be a part of: the awareness of and the ability to be humble. This is built on the presence of psychological safety: the shared belief that a team is safe to be themselves without fear of judgement. This is a major driving factor that connects people in a team. If we have people who are uniquely connected working with the same guiding principles, we can create vigorous teams with great depth. The parameters applied to internal or external teams are simple, yet not easy.

Typically, a project starts with the project manager- the captain of the team. It may not be your fault that some of the project parameters are less than desirable. It is most certainly your responsibility to be engaged and fix them.

As a project manager it is very important to have a strong team dynamic. One way to lead the team is to set boundaries. For example, work by creating an operating system on the pillars of authenticity, vulnerability and transparency - which are designed to illustrate a very humanistic approach to project management.

To keep it succinct- Choose to **BE HUMBLE.**

Adopt a humbled approach to the way you embark on leadership.

<u>A humbled project manager radiates the following</u>:

Generosity- We are here to be of service to clients, to stakeholders and most importantly, to team members. Be generous with your words, your thoughts, and your actions.

Be Genuine- Say what you mean; do not say it 'meanly'. Show people how much you care, because they matter. Create atmospheres to help foster great people.

Express Gratitude- I have read some neuroscience studies which reveal that gratitude releases oxytocin into the body. If oxytocin is present, cortisol is not. Your brain cannot allow negative thoughts to enter, when oxytocin is present. Expressing gratitude is good for everyone. Think back to a time when you received unexpected praise. Remember how great it made you feel? Make it real, make it about others. Be thankful.

Curiosity- Actively listen to people, and demonstrate mental hygiene. Ask questions to challenge assumptions and find the truths. Create a framework of higher level thinking questions to encourage continuous improvement. Curiosity leads to creativity and creativity leads to problem solving.

If you asked a young child to put on a shirt, and then walked away, how would you react when that child showed up with a shirt that was on backwards? There is a choice: to become emotionally distraught or to peel back the layers (through questions) to better understand the decisions that led to the outcome. The continuous inquiry paves the way to learn and to do better by thinking more clearly for the next endeavour, particularly for the project manager whom the message was intended.

Hold yourself to higher standards- If you are not going to demonstrate integrity, courage, authenticity and vulnerably, it would be unsound to expect likewise from those around you. Continuously elevate yourself. Never stop growing. Create the momentum and harness the energy to share with others.

The world we live in is fast paced, full of distractions and technological advances that are all pulling at our time and focus. At times, these elements can create unwarranted emotional reactions. The ability to ground myself and lead with a humbled approach has produced insurmountable gains in my career. This has most certainly augmented my project experiences, not only for me but all those around me. I invite you to embrace the knowledge to lead forward with a humbled approach.

CHOOSE TO BE HUMBLE

Many thanks for creating the space to allow me to share my story. You chose to be here to learn and continue to grow. It is with much respect that I express my gratitude to you as you move forward and enable yourself and others to be the best versions of yourselves. Never stop learning, leading and excelling.

JONATHAN CINELLI

Jonathan Cinelli is a Project Management Professional with nearly 20 years' industry knowledge in the electrical field. Jonathan demonstrates an incredibly specialized forward-thinking approach to business, designed for sustainability - with emphasis on continued growth and adaptability.

Jonathan's intuitive approach and collaborative problem solving has supported construction teams to achieve exceptional outcomes and set new standards. Utilizing the fundamentals of project management, coupled with his background in business, (electrical and brain-based coaching) Jonathan understands the critical components that lead to highly effective project teams.

Jonathan is an advocate for lifelong learning and truly enjoys sharing insight and knowledge with others. When not immersed in coaching children, Jonathan, a husband and father of two who is deeply in love with his family, spends the remainder of his leisure time at their home in Toronto.

Jonathan Cinelli, PMP, ACC, 309A
Director- Multi-Residential Projects,
OZZ ELECTRIC INC.
Concord, Ont
jacinelli@gmail.com
416-717-4139

THE SEVEN QUESTIONS OF CHANGE

PETER DE JAGER

While change initiatives crash and burn, for many reasons, the single point of failure is often merely: poor communication. We find change, especially that which *might* negatively affect us, threatening. Good 'communication' transforms "might" to "won't", and our fear of negative outcomes, to anticipation of working towards something better.

We know this. Ask managers what they need to do, to positively affect the outcome of a change? They respond, "Communicate! Communicate! Communicate!" This alliteration isn't wordplay. It is an unexpected response, repeated dozens of times when 300+ managers where surveyed on effective change management strategies. The repetition/emphasis on "Communicate" was deliberate. As managers we know that communicating is important. We also know the quality of the communicated information is critical.

Responses become less certain, more ambiguous, when we ask, "What exactly should we communicate?"

Obviously, different change initiatives present different issues. It might seem that communication strategies *must* vary wildly from one to another. Each change is unique to the individuals affected, the change, organizational culture, the current status quo, anticipated outcome and so forth. Superior communication is vital, and based on this list alone, complicated.

There is another approach to communication. Rather than communicating what _we_ think people should know about the change, we can communicate what we already know _they_ want to hear. The difference, while subtle, is powerful.

When faced with a change, there is a small set of questions to which we _all_ want answers. These questions do not differ much from one change to another – our answers to this set of questions will differ depending on the earlier variables – but the core questions stand firm.

These are those core questions, which can define the foundation of a communications framework for any Change;

1) WHY?

This is the winner, the key question- it is almost the only question worth discussing - if someone asks us to move from one side of the room to the other, or to stop using system 'X' in lieu of system 'Y', our response is always the same. "Why?" Understanding why a change is necessary is the most important question we have about any change. Without a good answer, we are reluctant to do anything different.

There are lots of good answers to the "Why?" question. One good one is... trust. If I trust you and you ask me to do something, my trust in you might be enough to prompt me to change. If that trust does not exist, you may ask yourself, then the reason for change had better convince us, or we are not moving from our safe and comfortable status quo.

There are two aspects to this simple "Why?" question;

1. Why should we change?
2. Why *this* change instead of that change?

2) WIIFM (WHAT IS IN IT FOR ME?)

Most organizations respond, "It's not about you!" How effective is this approach? How well do we respond to that answer?

The WIIFM question is a selfish one. When faced with change, we immediately focus on how it might affect ourselves. If it means we might get laid off, moved out, lose power, lose our title, responsibility, or must work harder - to name a few - we need to know.

Unless, we address this question - Even if it is to say, "We don't know," it won't go away. It will block any other information we might offer, until we address it.

The best way to think of the WIIFM question is as a nasty, viscous guard dog, blocking the gate to our attention. Until that dog is thrown a bone, no information about the change, sometimes not even the answers to the "Why?" question, are getting through to our reasoning process.

3) MONDAY?

Once we know how we will be affected. Now we want to know exactly when it will happen, and how exactly we will be affected. As in, "If the new payroll system is active on Monday, what will I be doing differently?"

It is a fair question. If we want people to change, we must describe what they are going to do differently in terms that everyone can understand. If we can't, then our vision is flawed and unattainable.

4) WON'T?

This question is a cheat. I rarely hear "What won't change," asked. Yet, it is an important question for managers to address, so I have added it to the list.

Imaginations are powerful, and what do we do when we don't have all the information? We speculate about what is missing, and we do what prudent people do. We imagine the worst that could happen, and then waste energy, and focus, worrying about the monster under the bed.

One goal of a change manager is to reduce anxiety – to stop needless worry – we can effectively do that by filling in the blanks instead of letting the imaginary monsters run loose.

An example: When the accounting system is replaced, we are still going to report to the same boss, earn the same pay cheque, and receive the same benefits. In fact, most of our *Status Quo* will remain the same, regardless of the size of the change.

5) MIGHT?

Change rarely goes smoothly – ask anyone who has ever coped with a new payroll system, especially government systems. People are aware, and we may have good memories, but things still go wrong.

The worst thing we can do when heading into the uncertainty of change is to insist that nothing can go wrong which quickly communicates to those around us that we have not really thought this through. People will benefit from our risk management strategies because often, people assume things will go as planned. However, this is not always the case.

6) WILL?

The 'First Law of Change' is that it involves a learning curve. Riding a bike, learning a new language, selling into a new market, marketing a new product – there are learning curves everywhere we turn. Even when we pay close attention to training, support, and fall-back positions, we are going to make mistakes. Then, productivity will decline, and things will go wrong.

If we pretend that the change is painless, that it is transparent to the user, then people know we are lying, or at least overly being optimistic.

So, when communicating change, highlight what will be difficult, what might cause concern, and then identify how you will address those things when actually arise.

7) SIGNPOSTS?

Change does not always happen quickly, it is often slow, almost glacial in nature. So, what happens without feedback on our progress? We lose both the motivation and the will to make sacrifices to move forward. The question is, "How do we know we are succeeding in our efforts?"

These are not the only questions we need to answer during a change, but they are crucial ones, and if the answers are not forthcoming? Neither will the change.

Who is "they" - They provide an exceedingly simple, yet powerful framework for communicating change. Knowing the questions and their answers in advance will prepare us for those difficult and stressful announcement meetings. Not knowing how we will answer them when they get asked, because they do get asked, ultimately sets us up for failure.

How to design a communications strategy:

Tip: Do not create a seven slide PowerPoint and address them in sequence. Instead... create what you would normally create to communicate the change.

Then...stick the questions on the desk in front of you and step through your intended communications as you read each slide, each sentence, and each sample of communication... and ask yourself --- "Which question am I addressing here?" Then make a tick mark next to the question you are addressing.

When you're done, your collection of tick marks, questions by question, or lack thereof, will point to where your communication plan needs work.

The flow of our communication is imperative. The notion of a seven slide PowerPoint is not the way to communicate change. It is too rigid a structure. Having said that, addressing the questions in the sequence listed is not a bad idea – the answer to each question leads the listener to the next question on the list. Instead of the seven slides why not tell the story of how it was decided that change was required?

The questions are not random – they follow our natural thought process when we are deciding to change. First, we decide why a change is necessary, then which change out of all the possible options (The two aspects of "Why?"). We determine how the change will affect us (WI-IFM), and then we figure out what we will need to do differently. We know, as the designers of the change what will not be affected. (Won't?).

We perform risk management as part of our thinking (Might?), and we plan how we will acquire the new skills (Will?) We know when we will have achieved our goal (Signposts?).

The strength within the 'Seven questions of Change' is simply this; it echoes the thought process that determined the change was necessary in the first place. By structuring our change communication around these questions – we are sharing the entire decision-making process with high hopes the listener will follow our reasoning, and 'get on board' the change.

© 2019 Peter de Jager – Peter is a keynote speaker/consultant who focuses on Change Management. You can contact him at pdejager@technobility.com – you can view much of his work at www.vimeo.com/Technobility

PETER DE JAGER

Peter de Jager is a keynote speaker/writer/consultant on issues relating to managing change of all shapes and sizes in all types of organizations. He has published hundreds of articles internationally on topics ranging from Problem Solving, Creativity and Change to the impact of technology covering areas such as privacy, security and business. His articles have appeared in The Washington Post, The Wall Street Journal, The Futurist and Scientific American.

He is best known to IT and Fortune 500 audiences for his efforts to create responsible awareness of the Year 200 Problem - Y2K issue – for which he received several awards from IT associations and Govt. Agencies.

In addition to presentations and seminars on the topics above, Peter has written dozens of regular columns in various publications. These have included; Association Trends, CIPS across Canada, Enterprise, Globe & Mail online and Municipal World.

He has spoken in 45 (and counting) countries and is recognized worldwide as an exciting, humorous, provocative and engaging speaker. His audiences have included the World Economic Forum, The World Bank and The Bank for International Settlements.

Peter's presentations and workshops are highly interactive, entertaining, irreverent to mistaken ideas and most distinctively - provocative. He positively encourages the audience, by demonstrating conflicts between their stated beliefs and behaviors, to think differently about what they thought they knew. You can view much of his work at - www.vimeo.com or contact him at pdejager@technobility.com.

Peter de Jager
Toronto, ont
Www.technobility.com
Pdejager@technobility.com
905-792-8706

THE VALUE OF A 30-60-90 DAY PLAN

PEG DUGGAN

*"Remember, you only have one opportunity to
make a strong first impression."*

[Unknown source]

Whether starting a new position, kicking off a new project, or leading a new project team, begin by creating a 30-60-90 day plan. When focused on early, this approach often wins and establishes a momentum of success to carry throughout your projects and career.

WHAT IS A 30-60-90 DAY PLAN?

Congratulations. You got the job, new position, or new project. A 30-60-90 day plan outlines what you will do in the first 90 days. It defines a strategy and the actions that accelerate the transition into your new role. During your first 90 days, you are building key relationships with your manager, team members, and the project's stakeholders. As a new player in the game, your first 90 days are critical for ongoing success. The 30-60-90 day plan makes that happen quicker and more effectively.

In his book, *The First 90 Days*, author Michael Watkins details how to develop critical success strategies and why it is important to do so.

31

The process starts by first assessing strengths, weaknesses, and vulnerabilities in you. Next, by looking closely at the situation, you develop an understanding of the opportunities and challenges in order to focus on the right approach with solutions in just a short time, establishing credibility and creating momentum.

While serving as a chapter leader for the Project Management Institute (PMI) New Hampshire Chapter, volunteer retention rates improved when each volunteer was assigned a peer mentor and was asked to complete a personalized 30-60-90 day plan. In this case, the 30-60-90 day covered these topics:

- Who is who?
- What do you need to know?
- Answers to frequently asked questions.
- How "It" works? For example: How a board meeting works, how to organize a chapter meeting, or how elections are run.

All New Hampshire Chapter volunteers received this as information during their first 30 days through a series of emails and links to internet pages. The peer mentor and volunteer completed and personalized the plan by adding more specific tasks, focused training sessions, meetings with key stakeholders, and set specific, role-related goals for the next 60 days.

The personalized 30-60-90 day plan gave volunteers the foundation they needed to perform their chapter role with confidence. They also felt appreciated and did not feel forgotten or left to fend for themselves after they raised their hand to volunteer. It was a win for the chapter and a valuable tool that reduced friction during the transition as volunteers moved into new roles.

If there is no 30-60-90 day plan during the onboarding process for your new role, develop your own. You can use one of the many available templates to guide you through the process which will allow you to tailor a plan according to your needs. Imagine creating a lasting impression with your new manager as you display initiative, eagerness to learn, and willingness to seize on the opportunity to become recognized as a team player by others in your organization.

GET READY, GET SET, GO!

But, why wait for your new role to begin? Why not start sooner than your first day? Western University offers a six-week Massive Open Online Course (MOOC) through Coursera.org called "Power Onboarding" which covers the development of personal on-boarding plans, also known as POPs. It starts well before the new role begins and uses a 90-60-30 day worksheet to layout an action plan. It is a framework which you tailor to you. Each stage focuses on three questions: how you work with others, what you know, and who you are.

CREATE YOUR PERSONAL 30-60-90 DAY PLAN

As you define the plan that will help you become successful in your new position, remember, this is an opportunity to make a great first impression. During the *Get Ready* stage you look 90 days ahead.

And, perform the following assessments as you build your repertoire of skills:

- Review previous experiences.
- Examine how you work with others.
- Identify your personality traits and skills.
- Assess your emotional intelligence.

- Solicit feedback from others.

At the *Get Set* stage, you look 30 days ahead and perform the following assessments as you continue to define how you work with others and fill gaps in your skills:

- Build a communications style that matches your boss, if possible.
- Read more about the position, expectations, rules, and culture.
- Identify who is on the team already.
- Educate yourself about the company, organization, and department.
- Update your image.
- Create a plan to manage impressions.

At the *Go* stage, on day 1, start with the right attitude, be resilient, and be willing to ask for help. Also:

- Find early wins and contribute.
- Stay focused on the goals you set.
- Observe group dynamics and culture.
- Look for mentors.
- Learn the process.
- Remember names.
- Network.

PLAN TO LEAD

Congratulations. You have been given the task to take over an existing project and team. I cannot think of anything scarier than stepping into a role previously filled by another project manager with a team that has already developed a working style and culture. Notice I did not say failing project or dysfunctional team. Regardless, any change in the team dynamics needs to be addressed appropriately irrespective of the project's status. As a project manager assigned to an existing team, the 30-60-90 day plan is a great tool that will allow you to become fully integrated into the team and project in a relatively short time.

As a project manager stepping into a project in process, you absolutely need a plan.

Key focus questions are:

- What do I need to know?
- Who do I need to know?
- What can I do for the team and project?
- What do they need to know about me and my expectations?
- How does the team work together?
- What are the team's strengths and weaknesses and what do they need to develop and succeed?
- What are the opportunities and challenges?
- Scheduled actions are:
- Observe the team – however, meet often and regularly to build relationships with your team members.
- Walk-about every day.
- Meet with stakeholders.
- Never eat lunch alone.
- Listen to what others have to say.
- Learn as much as you can, as quickly as you can.

- Share your Personal Leadership Philosophy (PLP).
- Identify anything else you can do in the next 90 days to make a positive impression on your team.

I am an introvert. My 30-60-90 day plan, together with my Personal Leadership Philosophy (PLP) enabled me to successfully lead projects, several times. This included stepping into the role as president of the New Hampshire Chapter. My PLP was created as a result of the "Leader's Compass Workshop" for Academy Leadership, taught by Jim Emerick. During the workshop, PLPs were discussed, and then built. My PLP includes:

- A statement of what leadership means.
- A list of personal values.
- Operating principals on how I plan to work.
- My expectations for the team and what the team can expect from me.
- My commitment as a leader.

My PLP is a deliverable on my 30-60-90 day plan that I share with my teams. It is also part of every operational plan I create. Again, the 30-60-90 day plan proved useful to my success and the success of the organizations I served.

A PROJECT WITHIN A PROJECT

Congratulations. You are assigned a new project which has lots of unknowns and uncertainty and, naturally stakeholders are concerned the project will fail. A 30-60-90 day plan is a project within a project.

It identifies in detail the target goals for the critical first three months of your project. Each month is one phase or stage. Using the 30-60-90 day plan is useful in this situation because it will provide enough data to determine if the project is on the right path or if it should be modified or canceled.

Start with a brainstorming session and use the results to complete an *Impact vs. Effort* analysis. You have just prioritized your list. The items with high impact and low effort, often referred to as low-hanging fruit, are what should be targeted for the first 90 days. The items with high impact and high effort probably require more resources and may take longer to complete. Nonetheless, they are important to the project; next on the to-do list - the items with low impact and low effort. The items with low impact and high effort may be put off till later or dropped. Then, focus the next 90 days on delivering the low-hanging fruit.

Here is an example: Let us say your organization is contemplating creating a Project Management Office (PMO). Begin by, creating a three-month pilot project using the 30-60-90 day plan to target early wins (low hanging fruit) from an Impact vs. Effort analysis. Take an agile approach and build a Minimum Viable Product (MVP) with artifacts, processes, and templates that you can start to use in 30 days, then add more in 60 days, and again in 90 days. Remove the uncertainty, get buy-in from your skeptical stakeholders, and create momentum to continue to build a successful PMO beyond the pilot.

BUILD MOMENTUM

There are many ways to use the 30-60-90 day plan, or 90-60-30 day plan, as a project manager. It is an important tool to include in your personal and professional tool kit. It focuses direction while targeting critical, easy, early wins. Combined with other project management tools, your plan builds momentum and project success.

I have only scratched the surface. There are templates for professional development, onboarding, sales plan, team building, team development, strategic plans, or succession plans. The list goes on. I am sure by now you have come up with your ideas on how you can use the 30-60-90 day plan.

The 30-60-90 day plan is a game-changer. Use it!

PEG DUGGAN

Peg Tesla Duggan, PMP, PMI-ACP, currently works as a project manager at the Diocese of Manchester and is responsible for managing several of the Bishop's Strategic Initiatives.

She has volunteered with the PMI New Hampshire Chapter since 2005 in various roles including Webmaster, Director of Technology, Director of Operations, and PMI New Hampshire Chapter President (2012-2013) and most recently, as VP Operations. In addition, she is also a member of PMI Maine Chapter since 2019.

She is also the founder, chief tinkerer, story-teller and Consulting Project Manager at MAD by Design offering web development, internet marketing, e-publishing and social media services to professionals and small businesses. Prior to this, she was the Windows NT Senior Software Product Manager for Digital Equipment Corporation and Windows NT Senior Software Product Marketing Manager at Compaq (now HP).

Peg Duggan, PMP, PMI-ACP
MAD by Design
Manchester, NH
https://www.linkedin.com/in/pegduggan/
pegduggan@gmail.com
603.801.1468

YOUR EMOTIONAL INTELLIGENCE: A POWERFUL TOOL THAT IS WITHIN YOUR REACH

SUSAN IRWIN

P M practitioners spend countless hours reading and researching ways to deliver successful programs and projects. In fact, a search of project management literature and class offerings yields over 5000 results to include processes, tools, and techniques that individuals within the project management field can use to implement successful projects. As PM practitioners, we continue to look for the Holy Grail for successful project delivery - is that not the purpose of lessons learned? We spend countless hours working with our teams to document and review what went well, and what did not, so we can avoid making the same mistakes on future projects. With all this research and work, why is it that project performance continues to decline (Pulse of the Profession 2019, 2019)? What happens if I told you the key to success is not a magic book, template, or technique but instead something you have in your toolbox already - something that enables you to continue to grow and expand. What happens if I tell you that the key to project success is emotional intelligence (EI)?

EMOTIONAL INTELLIGENCE

So, what is this EI concept? At the core, EI focuses on an individual's ability to use, understand, and control emotional information in real-time. If used correctly, EI can result in a high-performing employee, which can result in organizational success (Emmerling & Boyatzis, 2012; Goleman, 1995; Kunnanatt, 2012). EI makes three key assertions:

- Emotions are vital and play a critical role in your life.
- People do not use or manage emotions in the same way.
- People do not understand emotions in the same way.

It is safe to assume that based upon the EI assertions, individuals will not handle or adapt to situations in the same way. Let's stop here for a minute. Can you think of a time at home or during a project meeting when you delivered bad news, and two individuals handled it in two different ways? Maybe one individual was extremely emotional about the news – upset and frustrated, and the second individual was nonchalant about the situation – calmly stating "stuff happens." This is a real-world example of EI at play.

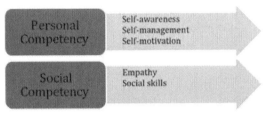

EI consists of five dimensions under two categories. Category 1, personal competency, included (1) self-awareness, (2) self-management or self-regulation, and (3) self-motivation. Category 2, social competency, included (1) empathy, and (2) social skills.

1. *Self-awareness:* Individuals who have high self-aware understand their emotions and how their emotions affect others and will often use their emotions to gain control of a situation. For example, PM practitioners are inundated with change every day – a change in the resource, a change in the timeline, a change in the scope. These changes need to be conveyed to the

team, but as a PM practitioner, do you deliver the news upset or with an overwhelming sense of calm? Most likely, you deliver with a sense of calm even though inside you are frustrated.

2. *Self-regulation:* After an individual has mastered self-awareness, they evolve to self-regulation where they learn to regulate their emotions. Individuals who understand self-regulation remain calm even in the most unstable situations.

   Think of a time when everything was going wrong. You are in the midst of a deployment, and it is not going as expected, and you cannot roll back. You are tired; your team is tired; do you get upset? Probably not, and why? Because you have mastered self-regulation. You know that if you become upset, the team will get upset and nothing will be accomplished.

3. *Self-motivation:* Motivation drives an individual to proceed with his or her goals even when there is a possibility of failure. How many times have you worked on business or technical requirements or some other tasks that are not in your wheelhouse? Yet, it had to be done? This is an example of motivation, taking on tasks because they must be done even if they result in possible failure.

4. *Social Awareness*: Individuals who have high social awareness tend to be empathic, understand that emotions can be both verbal and non-verbal, and provide emotional support to others as needed. As a PM practitioner, one of your primary responsibilities is to understand your team. Have you ever been in a meeting and you notice a primary resource with their

arms crossed and a less than happy look on their face? These individuals are demonstrating non-verbal emotions that can impact the emotions of others within the team. Emotions are like ping-pong balls; they bounce off each other and can impact the emotions of others. Think of a time when one person's emotions caused the team to become upset.

5. *Relationship Management*: Individuals who score high in the social skills quadrant recognize that it takes a team to complete a task and what is necessary to obtain results from others (Goleman, 1995). Rule number 1 in project management— there is no I in team. As a PM, you know the key to any success is that your team is operating as a well-oiled machine or in PM practitioner lingo, they are 'performing'. To do this, you need to ensure that relationships are maintained and that personal issues are addressed quickly.

FIELD OF PROJECT MANAGEMENT

Research in the field of project management has found that leadership skills of PM practitioners are instrumental to the success of a project (Aarseth, Rolstadis, & Anderson, 2014; Müller & Turner, 2010) and emotional intelligence (EI) is a critical component of leadership (Mersino, 2013). Why is this?

Projects have a defined start and end date. Because they have a specified end date, most project teams are more focused on completing a set of tasks to deliver the project on time, as opposed to building relationships, which can result in heightened emotions. Research has found that PM practitioners who possess high EI skills can solve challenges that are intrinsic within projects today (Clarke, 2010). In addition, companies implement projects as a way to address an organizational issue (PMI, 2013b), and during the management of the project, the project manager and the project team, is inundated with various problems such as (a) lack of resources, (b) technology issues, (c) organizational politics, and (d) scope creep. All of which can quickly fuel conflict within a team. It is the PM practitioner's responsibility to ensure the conflict does not negatively impact the successful implementation of a project.

Projects require PM practitioners who are willing to make a decision. In fact, according to PMI (2013b), a PM practitioner's ability to make decisions was identified as a critical skill by stakeholders. From a PM practitioner's standpoint, the act of making a decision, let alone a good one, can be complex and challenging when they are faced with uncertain information. This can result in a decision that is not only incorrect but also could cause further delays, cost overruns, and quickly frustrate employees. EI has a direct correlation between both reason and emotion and can have a direct influence over a person's thinking and decision-making process. This is because emotions contain key information about how a person feels about a specific issue or situation, which – if not suppressed – can help one make a better decision.

Finally, project managers are considered the leaders, the Chief Executive Officer (CEO), the quarterback of their project. Leaders serve at the bequest of their followers. This statement is never truer than in the world of project management because most PM practitioners do not have direct managerial authority over their team, in fact, a majority are appointed by those in charge, but for a PM practitioner to be successful, they must be both viewed and accepted as the project leader. Leadership acceptance is often accomplished through a mutual trust arrangement between the leader and the team. The leader will provide the team with what is needed (support, decisions, information) and the team will complete the work. Failure of the leader to live up to their end can result in a team that will lose trust in their leadership and will become unproductive.

EI is an essential component to the success of any project. As a PM practitioner, you are trained to use tools, templates, processes, and procedures to help ensure project success. In fact, for those that are certified, the project management practitioner (PMP) exam is centered on these concepts. These concepts are is not enough though. As PM practitioners you do not need to throw away the tangible deliverables that they have been accustomed to creating. Instead, you need to marry these deliveries with EI competencies. By understanding your emotions, the emotions of others, and by being more empathetic, you can become a more successful PM practitioner delivering successful projects.

SUSAN IRWIN

Susan Irwin is an experienced portfolio developer and project management practitioner, educator, and author, with over 20 years of experience in the field of project management. She manages portfolios, programs, and complex projects in the government, healthcare and business sectors. Susan started her career in technology as a software engineer and evolved to various professional positions, including Sr. Technology Program Manager and Portfolio Management Office (PMO) Manager. Susan has extensive knowledge managing projects using the waterfall, agile, and hybrid approaches and has experience implementing methodologies based upon the organization's needs. In addition to her vast experience as a practitioner, Susan is also an active volunteer for both the PMI and PMI CAC chapters where she most recently served as the chapter president. In addition, she serves as a volunteer instructor for multiple certification classes.

Susan holds several certifications in development, process improvement, project management, agile, and Scaled Agile Framework® (SAFe) and has been a member of PMI since 2005. Susan's education includes a Bachelor and Master's degree in Computer Science from Troy State University in Montgomery, a Master of Business Administration with an emphasis in project management from Florida Institute of Technology, and a Ph.D. from Capella University in information technology with an emphasis in project management. She currently resides in Birmingham, Alabama with her daughter and two dogs, Bailey and Maggie.

Susan Irwin, PhD, PfMP, PMP, ACP, SPI, CSM, LLGB
Birmingham, AL
https://www.linkedin.com/in/susan-irwin-phd-pfmp-pmp-pmi-acp-pmi-sp-ba82314/
susanmirwin001@gmail.com
334-462-7342

RISK IDENTIFICATION USING THE PREMORTEM TECHNIQUE

JOHN JUZBASICH

During risk identification, (brainstorming sessions) our natural optimism (Vaughan, 2000) plays a significant role and influences the process. People do not like to think negatively—we often overlook risks (now issues) that should have been identified earlier. Project teams want their projects to be successful so that optimism prevails. In order to do a better job at risk identification one must change the frame, which is the best technique to improve decision making as recommended by many scholars (Bazerman & Moore, 2009; Russo & Schoemaker, 2002; Kahneman, 2011).

The premortem is an excellent risk identification technique that can be used in project management, decision-making and as a brainstorming tool; it is a frame changer. Although the premortem has been described by Klein (2007) in Harvard Business Review and is mentioned by Nobel Prize Laureate Daniel Kahneman (2011), few project management or risk management textbooks refer to this decision improvement technique. In this chapter, I describe an exercise I developed for using the premortem technique to identify project risks and to train project managers on how to incorporate the premortem into their project risk management plan.

The first opportunity for me to test the technique was during a risk management class with the US Marines at their base in Albany, GA. The project manager of the project we used for the exercise was elated and left clutching his results. He told me that he was going to review the outcome with the base Commander. Within a month, I incorporated it into all my risk management, project leadership, and project management classes. Over the past few years, my team of instructors have delivered it to the several government agencies and departments, and various industries including pharmaceutical firms, companies of all sizes, for profit and non-profits, and many other organizations. I have also presented it at the PMI Mass Bay Chapter and in other project management venues.

The technique is a brainstorming technique, but with a twist. Like other brainstorming exercises, it ignites participants' creativity, ingenuity and imagination. During the risk identification process, we often use brainstorming to answer the question: What could go wrong? We are in the present peering into the future. Participants begin speaking out loud and create a list of their ideas. Unlike typical brainstorming activities, the premortem technique changes the tense from the future to the past, by asking: What did go wrong? We are now looking back at the past in order to see different risks that had turned into issues.

The premortem technique helps tame optimism in the decision-making process and provides excellent input into the risk management process. The procedure is quite simple: When the organization has come to a decision - to embark on a new project or business initiative, gather a group of individuals, about 20 if possible—they need not be familiar with the project and may come from different functional areas-distribute three to five Post-it® notes or 3x5 cards to the participants. Next, the project manager explains the project to the group.

After the project has been explained to the participants, the facilitator asks if everyone understands the project. They must be firm and not allow people to solve any problems; it is important that they encourage the group to focus on understanding the project at hand, nothing more. The facilitator turns the clock forward one year. If there is a clock in the room, the facilitator points to it; if not, they point to a watch and say:

> *"Imagine that we are one year into the future on __/__/___ [mention the date]. We implemented this plan as it now exists. The outcome was a complete and total disaster by any and every measurement, a real fiasco, a total train wreck." On your Post-it® notes (or cards) write out reasons for the failure. Write one reason per note (or card). Please remain silent during this process.*

Oftentimes there will be a few giggles, but the facilitator should emphasize that there is no talking or laughing permitted, the room should be silent allowing people to think. After five to seven minutes, each person reads one of their notes aloud; the facilitator circles through the group again and again until all notes have been read. No judgement is cast upon anyone's submission. However, there will be a few gasps and "Oh no's!" If a reason for failure is vague, the facilitator may ask for clarification.

The notes are collected and given to the owner of the project. The exercise might have been a bit embarrassing to the project manager; however, they are the recipient of a new set of project risks. These reasons for failure have now become identified project risks and the list serves as additional input into risks associated with the decision or project. Every time that I have conducted this exercise the project manager was thankful, and they obtained several significant new risks to incorporate into their risk management plan. The newly identified risks should be incorporated into the Project Risk Register and managed appropriately.

According to Kahneman, the premortem technique has three main advantages. First, the silence during the ideation phase forces one to think, using System 2, and reach deep inside one's memory for possible reasons for the project failure. Without discussing the project with others, the silence during the thinking period reduces groupthink, which affects many teams during the decision-making process regarding a project or business initiative.

Secondly, the premortem eliminates the "disloyalty effect" that often accompanies group decisions. Often, after a decision has been made, the participants may begin to feel uncomfortable with the decision. However, they dare not voice their concerns for fear of being labeled "disloyal" to the endeavor. Therefore, individuals are reluctant to share their reservations about the decision and proceed with the project or initiative despite their misgivings.

Lastly and most importantly, by re-framing the matter from the future to the past, the premortem unleashes the imagination and knowledge of the individuals in this important direction. *What could go wrong?* Was changed to: *What did go wrong?* The premortem technique has proven to be invaluable in project risk identification, in that traditional risk analyses look forward—into the future. By simply changing one word from "could" to "did" - for instance, the facilitator changed the frame of the discussion. In doing so, the brain's power is unleashed in a new direction and the result is a new set of risks to be managed.

The premortem technique is a focal point in my talks and classes on project risk management. What is amazing is that it releases participants' imagination and they come up with new and incredibly different risks that could negatively affect the project. The technique provides a much-needed method to reduce unwarranted optimism in decision making and project risk management.

JOHN JUZBASICH

John Juzbasich, D.Ed. (ABD), MLD, PMP, is a partner at Merit Systems LLC, which performs instructional training for professional development, project management, and information technology in South America, Asia, Africa, the Middle East, Europe, and the United States. John is responsible for the Human Resource Development group, and he regularly teaches leadership and project management, designs instructor-led, web-based, video-based workshops, and develops training interventions and customized programs for corporations and government agencies. He leads internal projects at Merit Career Development, as he has throughout his previous work at IBM, UNISYS and other companies. He is also an adjunct professor at Penn State University in the MBA and MLD programs. John earned a bachelor's degree from the Wharton School of Business, University of Pennsylvania, a Master of Leadership Development from Penn State University, and is currently completing his dissertation for the Doctorate of Adult Education in Leadership at Penn State.

John Juzbasich, D.Ed.(c), MLD, PMP
Chief Executive Officer
Mobile: 610.613.1693
Office: 610.225.0477
jjuzbasich@meritcd.com

SOLVING THE RIGHT PROBLEM

LEONARD MARCHESE

OVERTURE

Before we start, imagine that solving a problem the way you did in the past is like standing in quicksand. Your only chance for survival is to grab the branch of new thinking. You grab it, extricating yourself from the quagmire. You let the new thinking fill your mind with an innovative approach to solving problems, overcoming challenges and thus seizing new opportunities. You share this unique approach with others in your organization. They realize and accept its soundness; they are inspired by your conviction; they commit to the new approach. You establish a foundation for forward movement. You create a cultural shift. You start a journey to achieve something exceptional.

Is this approach a little too abstract? Perhaps what I have learned is that helping clients solve problems for over 25 years is more concrete. Specifically:

- **It is common sense** – Solving the right problem produces the right results. Solving the wrong problem produces insignificant or irrelevant results.

- **Solutions create change** – Change impacts people. Gaining commitment early ensures greater success when the solution is implemented. Without commitment, inevitably there is re-sistance.

- **Naysayers have a voice** – A contrarian view may be a saving grace. Listen and understand naysayer perspectives; respond with compassion. If you are wrong, naysayers may help you make it right. If you are right, let the facts gain their trust and commitment. If ignored, naysayers are solution slayers.

- **Lead through serving** – Treat all participants and recipients as stakeholders. Understand, support and serve their interests over your own. Nurture this principle so it proliferates among participants and strengthens their commitment to one another. If you do not care, they will not care, and then you are stuck.

- **Stay relevant** – From beginning to end, the gold standard for successful problem-solving is to maintain a continuous razor-sharp focus on relevance—the relevance of the problem, the solution and the results. I have come to call this the Art of Relevance™. The moment you lose sight of what is relevant is when your results are in danger of becoming irrelevant.

- **Implementing the solution is the beginning** – Once deployed, it is time to realize the extent of the solution's value. How it is received, used, measured, supported and sustained determines the duration of your success beyond implementing the goal.

What I have enjoyed the most about my journey is the creative tension of challenges and learning to trust that the outcome will be new and worth the journey. Let us create your new problem-solving journey.

INTRODUCTION

Are you solving the right problem?

Before you answer the question, I ask you to do the following:

1. Read this chapter.
2. Consider the techniques.
3. Let me know your answer.

Send your response to len@rethinkinc.com.

Why should you care?

Solving the wrong problem inevitably results in inconsequential outcomes that have a serious impact on the organization and who it serves. This can lead to higher costs to resolve the real problem and implications of a deficient solution.

This chapter helps you understand how to solve the right problem and achieve exceptional outcomes by...

- Knowing you are solving the right problems and solving them to make a difference.
- Engaging the right individuals with the skills and attitude needed to solve problems.
- Recognizing, defining, substantiating and committing to solve the right problems.

- Ensuring solutions are relevant, viable, exceptional and sustainable.

SOLVING THE RIGHT PROBLEM

What are the main reasons for failure?

Frequently, the past determines how problems are perceived and solved in the present. This is a major error. The solution to a problem should create something new, and new means change. Change requires new thinking. Understanding those changes and their impact is part of defining the solution.

Problem-solving failures can be divided into two groups:

1. Jumping to problem-solving before fully understanding the problem's root cause and not establishing a clear and definitive problem statement. The effects of these shortcomings are well-known; they directly contribute to costly unsound decisions.
2. Unsound decisions are not only the result of not understanding the problem, but they are also the result of not using common sense in how data are interpreted and applied.

Contributing factors to solutions that fail to deliver expected results are:

- False assumptions – Making assumptions that are not factual, relevant or certain.
- Poor definition – Defining the problem inaccurately or similar to a past problem.

- Poor understanding – Neglecting to ascertain or properly interpret the root cause.
- Selfish decisions – Providing direction based on bias, domineering or self-serving motives.
- Erroneous conclusions – Using unreliable data and/or performing flawed analysis.
- Deficient solutions – Creating solutions that do not resolve the problem.

How do you avoid failure?

Ensuring the right problem is being solved is just the beginning. Even a properly defined problem statement requires validation that: a) it is worth the investment to solve; b) it has strategic importance; and c) it provides benefits to the organization while fulfilling recipients' needs. Apply this problem-solving checklist to achieve exceptional results. The checklist, below, incorporates aspects of Rethink's patented approach for problem-solving and innovation.

1. UNDERSTAND THE MOTIVATION

- Identify the facts worthy of further investigation.
- Connect the facts with the people and things affected.
- Analyze the data, its source(s) and what it implies.
- Solve disparities for a comprehensive interpretation.
- Evaluate the certainty of the problem and its impact.
- Confirm findings through collaboration and feedback.

2. PLAN THE DIRECTION

- Formulate the problem statement.

- Identify the problem's root cause.
- Determine if it is an existing or new problem.
- Research whether others previously solved it.
- Define the scope and significance.
- Substantiate the problem statement.
- Endorse the problem statement.
- Generate ideas for possible solutions.
- Obtain resources and commitments.

3. DEVELOP THE SOLUTION

- Combine related ideas.
- Select ideas to consider.
- Test assumptions, facts and implications.
- Characterize target recipients and dynamics.
- Engage external evaluations and feedback.
- Shape and evaluate solution options.
- Assess risks, constraints and dependencies.
- Estimate the strategic reach and range.
- Establish capability and capacity to fulfill.
- Prioritize and select the most relevant solution.

4. DEPLOY THE SOLUTION

- Communicate the challenge, solution, impact and benefits.
- Define success as positive evaluation from solution recipients.
- Include and respond to the voices of supporters and opponents.
- Help others visualize how they benefit from the solution.
- Secure commitments needed to support the solution.

- Establish the resources and processes to sustain the solution.
- Implement processes for maintaining relevance and value.

5. MEASURE THE RESULTS

- Evaluate internal support and external acceptance.
- Cultivate and support solution adoption.
- Assess benefits realized and value delivered.
- Analyze feedback and make adjustments.
- Compare actual to expected results.
- Determine root causes of any variances.
- Implement processes to gain insight.
- Gauge the need to reinitiate problem-solving.

Who Solves Problems?

Individuals who:

- Think creatively and strategically.
- Commit to solve the right problem.
- Grasp the impact and opportunity.
- Differentiate facts from falsehoods.
- Reject biases and ulterior motives.
- Manage change and resistance.
- Strive for excellence and significance.

When can you claim victory?

Solving the problem is the beginning. No matter how much the business celebrates, if the solution does not integrate, recipient dissatisfaction and dissociation often result in solution failure.

You need to be relevant from the outset. Data overload can overwhelm and confuse decision makers and the analysts supporting them. Predictive and guiding insights are needed to ensure you are not only solving the problem, but fulfilling the recipients' needs.

Problem-solving is a continuum. A business that makes offers rather than waiting for orders to fill understands that victory is not an endpoint; rather, it is the beginning of overcoming the next challenge, seizing a new opportunity, creating something exceptional.

How do you ensure that your problem-solving continuum triumphs?

Apply the Art of Relevance™. Whatever enters and proceeds along the continuum must hold true.

1. Reflection – Learn from your past. Apply what is relevant to creating new opportunities.
2. Re-examination – Deal with facts. Apply common sense and make relevant decisions.
3. Rejection – Eliminate falsehoods. Apply truths that offer the greatest value to recipients.
4. Recognition – Substantiate reality. Apply analytics to discern what is and is not relevant.
5. Root Cause – Apply root cause analysis to determine a relevant solution.
6. Relevance – Correlate problem and solution. Apply scenarios that test the relevance.
7. Resolution – Define the goal. Apply visualization and metrics to fulfill relevant results.
8. Realization – Delight recipients. Apply sustainable means for meeting relevant needs.

Implement this process to solve the right problems.

CLOSING THOUGHTS

Use what you learned from the past to improve your future through continuous improvement using this new approach to problem-solving.

Explore what has not been done and reverse think.

Discover what is not –versus what is. Create a new offer, and be surprised what exceptional goals can be achieved!

LEONARD MARCHESE

Creator, consultant, mentor, writer and speaker, Len Marchese launched Rethink in 1992 with a mission to help clients create something exceptional. His passion is creativity and innovation; he is inspired when clients say, "Wow! Nobody thought of that!"

Len brings clarity, candor and commitment to help clients overcome challenges, embrace change and seize new opportunities. His process for problem-solving and innovating is so unique it is patented.

A committed professional, Len has mentored numerous individuals new to project management. He is also known for mentoring some beyond the initial career stage, providing insights and guidance at an ever-increasing level of sophistication and complexity.

Len has a Certificate in Project Management from Boston University and has been a certified PMP since 2010. He served on the PMI review sub-committee for the PMBOK 5th Edition released in 2013.

Len has engaged audiences in numerous formal presentations and panel discussions at PMI Chicagoland Knowledge Sharing, ProjectTalks Chicago, IIBA Chicagoland, PM/BA World Conference, American Society of Trainers & Developers, Society for Human Resource Management, Columbia University, Cornell Club and Asia-Pacific Executive Banking Conference, among others.

Professionally and personally, Len strives to be true to his work and to himself, as well as to colleagues, clients, friends and family.

Len Marchese
https://www.linkedin.com/in/lenmarchese
len@rethinkinc.com
(312) 730-4184

GET DONE AND HAVE MORE FUN!
A rebel PM™s guide to adding play to build high-performing teams FAST!

NANCY MAYER

To succeed as a project manager — and even more so as a scrum master — one of your biggest roles is that of servant leader for your team and stakeholders. This begins with a shift in mindset. Robert Greenleaf best defines this:

> "A **servant leadership mindset** is one that begins with the desire to serve by meeting the needs of others."
>
> Robert Greenleaf,
> founder of the modern servant leadership movement

Over the years, I have found that project success happens when people feel heard, appreciated, and when their needs are met. Most importantly, success happens when people are happy. A positive environment encourages engagement. This fosters fulfillment and motivation, which results in increased productivity and satisfaction. Team members privy to these benefits and accept deeper ownership of their work. A built-in support system with collaboration and accountability from a true sense of community and care arises. The key is to design your project like a community; focus on the reciprocity of what a team does for a company and what a company can do to meet a team's needs. Dig deep and serve your teams on many levels: physically, emotionally, mentally, and even spiritually.

My success secret to helping teams create this type of community and quickly go from "Forming" to "High-Performing" is by introducing **PLAY** throughout the project.

Play is essential for success in business and project management. For instance, when children play there are three main benefits:

1. Play leads to creativity, which leads to innovation. The result is creative and innovative solutions.
2. Play helps children build their problem-solving muscle. Every business and every project is about solving problems.
3. Play helps children with socialization. We need to find fun ways to stay connected in an increasingly disconnected world.

In a growing engagement economy needed to unite four generations of team members, gamification is your **WIN** to an engaged project team.

A good definition for gamification is...

"The process of adding games or game-like elements to something (such as a task) so as to encourage participation." *Merriam-Webster dictionary*

To truly understand the benefits of using game thinking and gamification, it comes down to changing the conversation and getting past biases to have more interactivity, innovation and connection. I believe gamification is more than just leaderboards and rewards. I like to break it down into three different levels:

- Behavior Modification (Challenge, Achievement, Reward).
- Collaboration (shared goal, rules, constraints and voluntary participation).
- Experiential (simulations that reveal interesting lessons).

Team building most often utilizes a combination of behavior modification, to increase motivation, and collaboration, to improve solutions. A well-structured game framework simplifies our working lives and helps to increase the focus on great results.

In this "Key to Success" chapter, we will first look at (some of the best in class) from the gamification area of thought-leadership and then we will explore which ones apply at different project stages.

Key tools for successful project collaboration and communication:

GAMES:

GameStorming
A toolkit for innovators, rule-breakers and changemakers
https://gamestorming.com
Innovation Games
Creating Breakthrough Products through Collaborative Play
https://www.innovationgames.com
Tasty Cupcakes
Fuel for Invention and Learning
https://www.tastycupcakes.org

SERIOUS PLAY:

Lego
A powerful tool designed to enhance innovation and business performance
https://www.lego.com/en-us/seriousplay
CPSI (Creative Problem Solving Institute)
A proven method for approaching a problem in an imaginative and innovative way.
http://www.creativeeducationfoundation.org/creative-problem-solving/

FUN FACILITATION:

Liberating Structures
Simple Rules to Unleash a Culture of Innovation
http://www.liberatingstructures.com
Management 3.0
The Future of Management and Leadership
https://management30.com

Which tool to apply and when:

INITIATION (CHARTERING & KICK-OFF)

Whenever possible, book a full day for your project kick-off. Interspersed with the details of the project or product, it is critical to the project success to have some fun team-building activities. Team members connect faster once they understand the other members as real people.

Ice Breakers

These are an engaging way to start any meeting and will increase the participant's energy and promptly create a constructive, positive environment. Something as simple as "tell us something about you that most people at work don't know," will create flourishing connections.

Self-Assessment

The more that we understand ourselves, the better we understand and work with others. "Motivational Movers," from Management 3.0, provides 10 cards that represent the main intrinsic motivators. The objective is to prioritize from left to right what motivates you most to what motivates you least. Then share your story with a partner. As the leader, I document the answers and use this information to help inspire a customized motivation for each person.

Team Agreements

Lego kits used to build examples of specific team behaviors provide many insights. Aim to focus more on the story they tell rather than on what they build. Watch how people organize their Lego bricks for keen insights.

Success Criteria

Whether it is a "definition of done" or other documentation, it is often interesting to look what made previous experience successful. "Appreciative Inquiries" from Liberating Structures, shares and acknowledges keys to success.

To aid the adoption of new ideas or changes consider bookending major milestones with Open Space Technology. This unique facilitated "UnConference" brings stakeholders together to discuss important issues. The group self-organizes around topics that are important to them. Most of all, you are using invitation versus mandate. Everyone has an opportunity to join the conversation, increasing buy-in.

PLANNING (SPRINT PLANNING)

To get the best solutions, challenge the status quo and prototype your ideas before you begin to execute. Validate your assumptions with the customer; they need to be involved in the design and requirements of any project or product.

Problem Solving: Within the CPS framework, use divergent thinking (consider as many ideas as possible). Use specific criteria to narrow options down with convergent thinking (what will drive the best results). Three exercises in the "Clarify" module are designed to make sure you solve the right problem first.

Customer–Centric: Innovation Games is about putting ideas into action. There are discovery games, shaping games and prioritization games all based on cognitive science that gets your customers to tell you what is really important to them in an unbiased way.

EXECUTION (SPRINTS/DEMOS)

Here, the rubber meets the road, and the work gets done. Using more behavior modification models can increase speed of implementation.

Motivation: In his book *Drive*, Daniel Pink talks about the three things that motivate people: Purpose, Mastery and Autonomy. Co-create the purpose of the project in the kick-off, and a big shift in attitude will emerge when everything is in context. When it comes to mastery, watch and ask your team members what is important to them.

Explore rewards and ensure that they are in alignment with what motivates individual members. For autonomy, make sure everyone understands the expected results and then let them do them any way they want – this encourages innovation.

Collaboration: A team that laughs together works. Every day I assign one of the team members to bring two–three minutes of funny videos to play the next morning. The meeting kicks off on a positive note, and members learn about a person by what they find funny. This is one of my secret weapons. There are also some great liberating structures to have collaborative team conversations like WINFY (what I need from you).

CLOSE (RETROSPECTIVES)

At the end of a project (or a sprint), there are great opportunities for learning, recognition and celebration. A wrap-up party with some games and rewards is a fantastic way to finish any project.

REVIEW

I generally use both innovation games and tasty cupcakes for great wrap-up and retrospective ideas. You do not want to repeat the same thing over. One exercise we love is "Walk the Line" where you take a rope and walk through the highs and lows of the project.

CELEBRATION

Throughout the whole project, celebrate all wins. Achievements and rewards will release dopamine, and this will then increase the desire to keep achieving. This is one of the reasons teams can quickly increase velocity of delivery.

RECOGNITION

The little things count. Acknowledging your team members publicly is powerful. Once at a project's end, we had no budget for the party so I printed off fun certificates recognizing the team and put them in frames. To this day, several members still hang their certificates proudly in their offices.

Through laughter, deeper conversations and lots of celebration, you will have a high-performing team that looks forward to deliver every time.

It is simple - Happy people are more productive!

"Play BIG – Win BIG"

NANCY MAYER

Nancy Mayer is a Project Manager, Agile Coach and Business Strategist based in Toronto, ON and Salt Lake City, UT.

Nancy's company, Power Play Productivity Solutions, was created to help businesses increase productivity and project delivery by allowing leaders to take back their power, empower their people and create a positive, collaborative work environment where people are playing at their best.

Drawing on her 25 years of experience in project-oriented industries like business development, artist and event management, manufacturing and marketing and most recently, software development, she provides a variety of project management and facilitation services.

She is a recognized speaker and author and is known as a thought leader for three key foundations: Visual Thinking (canvases, mapping), Design Thinking (Prototyping and validating business ideas), and Gamification (using game design and thinking to make work engaging and fun).

She has a unique toolbox that combines traditional credentials (MBA, PMP, Masters Certificate in Project Management, Certified Scrum Master, Professional Scrum Master) to cutting-edge methodologies

(Innovation Games, Management 3.0, CPS (Creative Problem Solving), Liberating Structures) that lead to a positive impact on the bottom line.

She is an avid evangelist for the latest business tools and techniques that lead to collaboration and innovation. She is also passionate about "Getting the Customer in the Game" and runs highly effective CABs (Customer Advisory Boards).

She is as active in her personal life as she is in her business life and loves adventure and "calculated risks" like extreme skiing, and motor-cycles.

Nancy Mayer, MBA, PMP, CSM/PSM
Power Play Productivity Solutions
Toronto, ON / Huntsville, UT
https://www.linkedin.com/in/nancymayer13/
nancy@PowerPlayPS.com
www.MeetNancyMayer.com
801-388-3319

EMOJI LEADERSHIP: CONNECTING WITH THE NEXT GENERATION OF PROJECT TEAMS

LIAM PAUL MCKERACHER

"We need to talk..." Wait. What? If you were to receive this text or email message, your mind would immediately start racing. Although the sender's intent could be to simply spark a conversation later in the day, you might immediately assume the worst.

Even if "we need to talk" is marked by different punctuation the message still induces stress. There are only a few types of punctuation to formally end a sentence and convey meaning: a period, an exclamation point and a question mark. No matter what punctuation you use, the phrase "we need to talk" is likely to raise blood pressure — unless! — you string together a few punctuation marks to create the beloved little smiley-face :)

I advocate for digital forms of written emotion in day-to-day project communications — emoticons, emojis and bitmojis. Now, the phrase "we need to talk" becomes more calming with a smiley face: We need to talk :) Here, I am using an emoticon. Emoticons use an arrangement of punctuation as shorthand for a facial expression. In 2011, Apple's iOS5 release included a collection of small pre-set images that can be used in text and email communications. Dubbed emojis, these images draw their name from the Japanese for picture and moji for character (Troiano & Nante, 2018). They include facial expressions, caricatures, symbols, and even a pile of very happy poop. 💩 Emojis can be used to convey all sorts of different ideas in text communications.

Most PMs agree that successful project communication is challenging. We need to be clear and concise while sending a high volume of messages. Conversely, we need to tailor our communications to our stakeholders while providing a personal touch. Effective PMs know that you can rush tasks, but you cannot rush your relationships.

I started my practice of using emoji's early in my career after I learned that a project team member interpreted my short and often directive emails as angry and critical. Although I was simply trying to provide clear and concise direction, it was not received this way. In a 2007 study, Byron and Baldridge examined emoticons in business communications, and found that in an email without any emotional cues, such as emoticons, the receiver tends to project their own emotions onto the sender. A quick conversation cleared up the misunderstanding and I began to use emoticons to tailor future communications with greater sensitivity. However, as PMs, we often find ourselves in large teams, nestled in even larger organizations, and we need to continuously communicate in all directions. In complex institutions, the opportunity to tailor communications and have face-to-face conversations becomes challenging. Again, something as simple as a smiley face can help :)

I do not advocate straying too far from smiley face emoticons or plastering every email with emojis in work communications. Nor should direct feedback be softened with an emoji: "This does not meet the requirements. You need to redo this work :)" The smiley face may come across as insensitive rather than amiable. In this case, try speaking directly to the individual to clarify any misunderstandings around the standard of work.

Another pitfall of emoji communication is the use of symbol emojis, without understanding their cultural meaning. There is a language and subtext to some emojis which may violate your organization's code of conduct. For example, winks are ambiguous in real life. They are ambiguous in text too ;) See? It made that sentence weird. :-\ Be cautious and stick to conveying basic, work-appropriate emotion.

As with any communication tool you need to learn to use it appropriately. Right person. Right situation. Right time.

Millennials are not just entering the workforce. Increasingly, they are the workforce. Millennials hold prominent positions on project teams and, in many cases, are leading top-profile projects. Michael Dimock (2019, Jan 17) from the Pew Research Centre explains that "anyone born between 1981 and 1996 is considered a Millennial" (n.p.). This generational cohort has grown up emailing, messaging and texting. They have developed fluency in digital communications and are comfortable using more than just words to convey meaning. They expect digital fluency in return and are sensitive to how digital communications are crafted. A simple period has meaning and can cause hours of angst around the intention and the state of mind of the sender.

A great leader understands their team and shows this through empathy. In the late 1990's, Daniel Goleman introduced the idea of emotional intelligence. Goleman (1998) theorizes that successful leaders have emotional understanding of themselves and of their team. Essentially, a leader with a high level of emotional intelligence is aware of how they act when they are frustrated or upset, and are able to sense and respond to emotions in others. Goleman explains that, "if you're enthusiastic, energetic, optimistic, then people in the group will respond in kind" (p. 20). An emotionally intelligent leader will create a positive emotional response through their communications and build the team's comfort and trust with every opportunity.

The use of emojis help to show recognition for a job well done. Recognition should be timely and personalized in order to make the desired impact. On any project, it's a good strategy to make time to provide positive feedback to the team and their functional managers by email. It is also recommended to put team members' names forward for appropriate organizational recognition programs. However, these actions do not necessarily give a team member immediate gratitude and are not necessarily appropriate to the level of work they had contributed. Therefore, do not hesitate to send a quick "Great Job :)" or even a 'bitmoji' to express gratitude for a job that is well done.

Bitmoji is a smart-phone app and Google Chrome extension that allows users to build a personalized emoji or avatar. The app creates a library of 'bitmoji' images simulating the user's cartoon likeness. With the app installed, a user can scroll through the pre-generated images and append them to texts and emails.

We often hear in the workplace that leaders do not take the time to say thank you. A bank of "thank you" images is quick and effective. A well-timed bitmoji brings a smile to a team member's face and the personalized likeness of their leader goes beyond by simply writing – "Thanks."

Remember, this is only one type of recognition and does not replace a personally-delivered verbal thank you or ensure that your team's work is recognized more formally through rewards and compensation. However, for a task well-done during your team's day-to-day, this can have a great effect.

Some will argue that an emoji in an email will make the sender seem less competent or even professional. However, the importance of emotional intelligence in the workplace is trending, as is greater empathy in leadership. Emoticons, emojis and bitmojis can all be used to display emotion through text and graphics. Employed with comprehension and compassion they can improve your communication and your project leadership. Not convinced? In 1936, Dale Carnegie offered some simple advice to anyone who is trying to influence without authority: Smile more :-D

LIAM PAUL MCKERACHER

Liam McKeracher is an elder-millennial and a Senior Project Manager with the Health Systems Information, Analysis and Reporting Branch of British Columbia's Ministry of Health. As a former Officer with the Royal Canadian Navy, Liam found that his true passion lay in creating complex plans and successfully carrying them out. This led him to the world of project management.

Liam initially completed his Bachelor of Arts degree from the Royal Military College of Canada. He earned his PMP in 2015. In 2019, he finished his Master of Arts in Interdisciplinary Studies from Royal Roads University with a research focus in project and change management. As a practiced facilitator, Liam has honed his teaching skills through mentoring Junior Naval Officers on ships at sea, teaching business and financial literacy skills to young adults, and exploring the art and science of project management concepts with PMP exam preparation candidates and university students.

Liam is actively involved in giving back to the Victoria community and his profession. Over the past few years, Liam has taken on progressive leadership roles with the Vancouver Island Chapter of the Project

Management Institute, and in July 2019 assumed the role of Chapter President.

Liam McKeracher, CD, MA, PMP
Victoria, BC
https://www.linkedin.com/in/liam-mckeracher-pmp-37821358/
liam.mckeracher@gmail.com
250-589-9195

MEETINGS THAT MATTER

JASON ORLOSKE

Wednesday at 2:00 represents, roughly, the halfway point of an average work week. It is when you take stock of what you have accomplished and what is left to do. However, my Wednesday at 2:00 represented the most frustrating and pointless time in my week; the integration program status meeting.

I was a project manager on a mergers and acquisitions integration team. The program manager had a weekly meeting with all project managers to, as he put it, "touch-base." The meeting was scheduled to last 1.5 hours. Each project manager was to give their update in no more than five minutes. Given there were only five project managers, that equals out to a maximum of 25 minutes of updates. Allow for an additional 10-15 minutes to ask questions and boom, a 35-40 minute meeting! I'd even round it up to 45 minutes for scheduling purposes. But, as Parkinson's Law states, work expands to fill the time available for completion. In this case, it was 30 minutes of productive meeting and one hour of unnecessary discussion.

Meetings. If done right, everyone benefits from the decisions made and actions to take to keep projects moving. If done wrong, they are pointless and take up precious time that could be used being productive.

In this chapter we will focus on the three parts of a meeting - before, during and after.

BEFORE THE MEETING

Have you ever walked into a meeting and the organizer starts by saying "I know we scheduled an hour, but we probably won't need it to get through the topics I have." Do you also get invited to meetings with no topic, goal or agenda? When you contact the organizer for distribution, they give you a very brief description that leaves you wondering why you are invited. Do not worry, you are not alone! These scenarios play out daily all over the world.

As a meeting organizer, there are two important questions to ask yourself before the meeting: 1) how much time is required to meet the objectives, plus a little more for open discussion and 2) what is the agenda?

What comes first, the meeting length or agenda? This is a bit of a chicken-and-egg situation because you may have agenda items but no idea how long it will take to cover them. You may also know some of the attendees are quite busy and do not have a lot of time. The best plan - this may be offensive to some - is to select the minimum amount of time to achieve the meeting goals. For topics that may be more complex, do not be afraid to ask someone for their opinion on meeting length in advance. Sometimes, what you believe will take more time, in reality could be very simple for the right attendees to solve.

The agenda is one of the most important tools when it comes to preparing for a meeting. It lets attendees know what to expect, who will be there and the goal of the meeting. The agenda should clearly state the meeting intent, answering the "Why are we meeting?" question. Make sure the intent is action-oriented and avoid words like "discuss" or "talk about." Meetings are discussions, so it does not need to be restated. Instead, use words like decide, prioritize or solve. These are descriptive and give attendees more information on what will be covered.

Below the meeting intent, list the agenda items in a bulleted list. These should also be clearly identified. If an attendee is responsible for bringing information regarding an agenda item, be sure to list their name. If you have a team member who enjoys talking, which we all do, do not be afraid to set time limits on each item. Some agenda items can be reviewed quickly, whereas others may be complex and require detailed conversations. Be aware of which is which and tackle the more complex first.

Once the intent and agenda items are set, look at the list of attendees. Are the right people in the meeting? Are there others needed to make decisions or provide information? Are there people invited who do not need to be there? Audit your attendee list and make sure only the right people are invited and available to come. If they are not, see if they can assign a delegate to attend to make decisions in their place.

Finally, as you prepare for the meeting, ensure it has any necessary audio and video equipment needed for presentations or having remote employees on the phone. Personally, I like rooms without windows as attendees may daydream or get distracted by things happening outside the room. Fewer distractions lead to greater engagement. For remote employees, select a teleconference system that is easy to use, provides global dial-in numbers for international attendees, and has the ability to share information on your screen.

DURING THE MEETING

If possible, get to the meeting room and/or open the conference line in advance of the start time. You never know when there may be a technical issue that could cause a delay. Also, as a project manager, more often than not you will find yourself playing both the facilitator and note-taker role. Be sure you are setup to perform both tasks by having any presentation and note taking materials ready.

As attendees join, document who is there as part of the meeting notes. Be respectful of everyone and start the meeting on time. If attendees are used to running late, explain to them that, going forward, your meetings will start promptly and you do not intend to review items already discussed for late arrivals.

If there are attendees who do not know each other, allow time for a quick round of introductions. Depending on the type of meeting, like a project team kick-off meeting, for example, icebreakers may be needed to allow team members to learn a little bit about each other.

Once the meeting has started and introductions are done, go over the meeting intent and agenda items. Highlight the importance of the meeting goal and let the group know anything not related will be added to the "parking lot" for consideration at another time.

Facilitating the meeting is an art, one that takes experience to develop. You will have a variety of personalities and engagement levels, ranging from non-stop talking to completely silent. Be mindful of body language and ensure everyone is engaged and provides input. Ask those who are quiet for their opinions and respectfully ask those who talk frequently to allow others their turn. If you have attendees on the phone, continually ask for their input as well. Instead of calling them out, instant message or text them intermittently and ask if they have any feedback they would like to share.

One of the most frustrating meetings to facilitate is one where no one talks and the only voice is that of the project manager. When a decision is required, the project manager will bring it up for consideration and provide options, to which the team will usually pick the first recommendation. There is no discussion or debate. In this instance, you need to "allow for loud." If you know this team is quiet, invite someone with differing opinions who can give alternative ideas. If that is not possible, I have been known to make a decision in a team meeting I know others will not agree with just to interject healthy tension into the room. I am not seeking conflict, but I am seeking lively conversation.

If you find the topic drifting away from the agenda, utilize the "Parking Lot." You do not want to stifle good ideas. If the topic does drift, recognize that the points being discussed are valid and deserve to be revisited another time. Document them in the meeting notes as a parking lot item for future consideration. Then, go back to the original agenda.

When it is time to end the meeting, review the agenda again. Ensure all points were covered and highlight the decisions made. If there are actions or follow-ups, assign an owner and due date. These will be added to the agenda for the next meeting.

AFTER THE MEETING

You had a great meeting! Decisions were made and actions assigned. Now what?

Meeting notes are an essential after-meeting task. Decisions need to be documented, actions and due dates reinforced with those assigned, and parking lot items communicated. All this should be done as soon as possible after the meeting so it is still fresh in everyone's mind.

With today's technology, meeting notes and follow-ups can be distributed in several ways. Each company, project management office, (PMO) or team - may have a different method. Be sure to know what is preferred and adhere to those guidelines. When it comes to action items, be sure they are communicated in the meeting notes and follow-up with the owner to ensure they are getting done.

CONCLUSION

Meetings. When done right, they are valuable and help drive progress on your project. When done wrong, they can be a waste of time. Make your meetings matter!

JASON ORLOSKE

Jason Orloske has more than 20 years of experience helping companies and teams bridge the gap between organizational strategy and operational excellence through effective project portfolio management. He has experience in the biotech, healthcare, retail and legal and regulatory sectors.

Orloske is an author, blogger and experienced presenter. He has a Master's in Project Management from the University of Mary in Bismarck, ND, where he also taught project management courses for three years. He holds a Project Management Professional (PMP) and Scrum certifications.

Orloske has been a consultant for Fortune 100 companies and owns his own consulting practice, through which he helps leaders and team members be more efficient and effective in meeting management.

Jason Orloske, MPM, PMP, CSP
Fargo, ND
https://www.linkedin.com/in/jason-orloske-mpm-pmp-csm-cm-44174a9/
btgconsultllc@gmail.com
701-566-9052

BECOMING RESILIENT

STEVE PIECZKO

W hy do some project teams successfully weather the storms of constant change, while others fail to meet their objectives after being faced with a single roadblock? Why have we not significantly decreased the percentage of IT projects that fail, despite all the advancements in information technology, training, education and certifications? What are we missing?

I define a failed IT project as one that never went live, or one that created considerable negative financial or resource consequences despite going live. If you ask a dozen project managers for the top reasons these projects fail, they will mention changing requirements, chasing a date, lack of support from management, poor resources, and too many distractions and so on. All of those may be true.

However, I consider two causes of project failures to be more important: project teams that fail to confront reality, and teams that lack resilience.

CONFRONTING REALITY

I have seen project teams spend four times the initial project budget before somebody recognizes the project is failing and a decision needs to be made: shut down the project, or keep investing in hopes of recovery? It is often difficult to confront the reality of an impending project failure, because it requires answering tough questions such as, "How did we get here?" and, "Who created this mess?"

In general, most failing project teams deny reality by assuming success is possible and the costs of a project rescue are reasonable. Confronting reality requires the project team to make an objective, unbiased assessment of the causes of failure and turnaround requirements. Sometimes, confronting reality requires you to admit project failure and move on. On the other hand – even when all signs point to failure – resilience can enable a project team to snatch victory from the jaws of defeat.

PROJECT TEAM RESILIENCE

It is human nature and a best practice to start with the questions, "How long will this take? What will it cost?" Unfortunately, there are almost always changes in the scope, resources and/or budget during the execution phase, making the project less predictable than first appeared.

That is when projects can begin to fail.

Dealing with project surprises requires building resilience into the project team. Let me give you an example to illustrate its importance. Your home's water heater stops working or starts leaking, so you call a plumber for an estimate. You hire the plumber who offers a low and predictable estimate – for instance, $500. Only an hour into the repair, the plumber breaks a pipe at the location of an old plumbing weld and causes a horrible mess. Your basement floor is now flooded and your carpet is ruined. You no longer care about the plumber's ability to predict a $500 cost – you just want him to make the rising waters go away.

If you and the plumber were a resilient project team, you might have avoided the flood by pointing out the old plumbing weld before he broke the pipe. Or, you might have noticed he was rushing and putting too much pressure on the pipe and asked him to slow down, which allowed him to notice the old weld and avoid breaking the pipe.

FIVE STEPS TO CREATE A RESILIENT PROJECT TEAM

I define a resilient project team as one that can deal with real-world ambiguity, changing requirements, poor leadership and less-than-ideal team composition and member capabilities. Despite these and other roadblocks, a resilient project team finds a way to meet its objectives and successfully complete the project. Over the past decade, I have been involved directly or indirectly in the rescue of more than 10 project teams that were failing. Here are the steps I have taken to build resilient project teams that bounce back from adversity.

1. Assess each team member. This is one of the first steps of a project rescue attempt. Do you have the right heads in the right hats? Do you need to recruit additional talent? This assessment should go beyond evaluating the "noisy members" of a project team who are reacting emotionally to the situation at hand. I recommend asking the following questions of each team member to create a spreadsheet depicting the team's Roles, Outcomes, Passion and Execution (R.O.P.E. assessment).

Roles: What titles were given to each team member? (For example, project manager, project sponsor.) Are any key roles missing? Do you have multiple people attempting to fulfill the same role?

Outcomes: What must this project achieve? Answers might include a positive experience across the company, delivering the project on time and on budget, lowering technical debt, and/or simply completing this phase so the team can reach the next phase of the project.

Passion: What is important to each team member on this project? Responses might include communications, quality of resources, creating focus, good requirements, and so on.

Execution: What are you good at? Team member answers might include project management, requirements, testing, creating alignment or focus. Again, look for and address team member gaps or expertise duplication.

Beyond your initial R.O.P.E. assessment, there is significant value in reassessing the team again – say, one month into the project. If you hear surprising changes in team member answers, you have an early warning of larger issues that can lead to project failure.

2. Address dysfunctional team dynamics. Avoid the natural tendency to focus all your attention on the project plan's immediate deliverables. In many cases when a project team is failing, the problem is hidden much deeper in dysfunctional team dynamics. Stand back and observe the project team before diagnosing problems and acting on potential solutions.

3. Reshape team member attitudes. Great project team leaders quickly recognize when individual team members are failing – and they understand failure is not a permanent condition. A great leader helps individual team members learn from a failure and grow their technical skills. Of course, that assumes an individual is not punished for a failure, and the project implications of allowing this type of smaller failure are not too costly to the enterprise.

In dealing with an impending project disaster, it is also important not to lose sight of the likely customer impact. Several years ago, I witnessed a project implementation plagued with massive problems that prevented the client from shipping customer orders over a period of several weeks. Countless meetings focused on fixing the software bugs and trying to forecast system recovery – until the leadership team recognized that the project team had lost sight of serving the end customer. Orders started flowing again when the project team was refocused on solutions that worked in the short term but were outside of addressing the key technical issues. This bought time for the technical team to implement a longer-term solution.

4. Strengthen team leadership. Too often, project managers leap to address the symptoms of a failing project – such as scope creep or lack of resources – when the root of the potential failure is hidden several levels deeper, in dysfunctional team dynamics. A great project leader knows how to quickly identify and address these underlying problems. You may need to find a new team leader if coaching a less experienced project manager is not working. Great project team leaders exhibit two important attributes:

Help team members understand, "What's in it for me?" Great project team leaders make a compelling case for team members to follow them. Do team members respect their project team manager? Ask how many of the team members previously worked on a project with their current leader. After all, no one wants to re-up for a problematic team leader.

Be the last to speak. Simon Sinek is one of my favorite Ted Talk contributors. He says that great leaders learn how to be the last person to speak. A great team leader asks for project team member ideas up front, rather than attempting to influence team members to adopt his or her previously stated recommendations. It does not encourage people to volunteer dissenting insights when their manager tells them, "We have a problem and I think we need to do the following . . . but I want to hear what you think." (Not.)

5. Invest in long-term team leadership success. Strong team leaders know they constantly need to evolve their leadership skills. They seek mentors who are willing to spend time to help them grow professionally. They learn by doing when they become mentors for other individuals. Do not be afraid to ask someone to be your mentor. Even the most successful business leaders have valued mentors. Former Columbia University football coach, Bill Campbell, is often referred to as "the most important executive you've probably never heard of" because he mentored Apple's Steve Jobs and Google's Larry Page, among others.

THE VALUE OF PROJECT TEAM RESILIENCE

It is human nature to want predictable results – and in a perfect world, the best-run project teams exhibit a high level of predictability. In the real world, success almost always requires a resilient project team that can confront the new reality when projects become less predictable. Have the right leader to drive the team forward, have the right heads in the right hats, and build in resilience to strengthen the team's ability to turn around a struggling project while learning from failures.

The value of project team resilience goes beyond the current project. It will benefit your next project, too.

STEVE PIECZKO

Steve Pieczko is a management consultant, software developer, published author and speaker on management consulting topics. Steve is a regular speaker on project management topics for organizations like; AT&T, PMI Chicago, PMI Michigan, the Technology Leaders Association, Project Summit BA World, The People Side of Software and The Agile Professional Learning Network.

Steve has consulted at several Chicago-land companies in Healthcare, Finance, Banking, Telecommunications, Transportation and Supply Chain which included rescuing more than 10 projects from eminent failure.

Steve's published articles include:

- Solve 'Intractable' Problems with Consultative Servitude
- Elevating the Bar on Customer Satisfaction begins with Sales
- How to Throw a ROPE to a Struggling Project
- When Projects Stall, Get the Right Heads in the Right Hats
- Can Artificial Intelligence Reduce Project Failures?
- Why You Need a SWAT Team for Failing Projects?
- The 3 Minute Mile, why is my project team killing itself?
- Waterfall? Agile? How About WetAgile?
- Who Lowered this Bar and Why Can't I Raise It?

- Dad, You can't Manage a Basketball Team, You're a Computer Guy

Steve is the founder of RelMap™ Consulting and ProjectRescue.us and BecomingResilient.com. RelMap™ Consulting is a Management Consulting company and ProjectRescue.us is a service of RelMap™ Consulting. For more information visit RelMap.com

AWAKENING OUR INNER EINSTEIN

SARAH RAMKISSOON AND
KRISTINA RIIS

"I have no special talent. I am only passionately curious."

(Albert Einstein)

What does curiosity have to do with project management? What we do is not rocket science. Should we not just focus on implementing what we know best?

Certainly, curiosity can get us into trouble, as both Curious George and Alice could attest!

However, curiosity driven by a thirst for knowledge and understanding has the potential to greatly benefit project leaders (and team members).

The very nature of project management brings together multi-disciplinary skills, knowledge and resources to create something unique. It is a difficult enough outcome, made even more so as business and technology environments evolve at an ever-increasing pace that shows no sign of slowing. As project delivery leaders, we rarely have the opportunity to opt out of that chaotic environment. It is critical to our success that we bring certainty, order and simplicity to that madness.

When we find ourselves in stressful circumstances, our amygdala (the region of our brain responsible for the "fight or flight" reflex) immediately kicks into high gear, bypassing the parts of our brain responsible for higher level information processing. We stop listening, our abilities to reason dwindle, and we cannot make complex decisions. This adds to our stress and to the stress of everyone around us, resulting in a negative feedback loop that makes the situation worse, as everyone else's amygdala fires up.

Happily, we can learn to leverage our innate ability to be curious to defuse the situation. According to Diane Hamilton, putting ourselves in a state of curiosity calms our hyper-excited amygdala (Hamilton, 2015). As leaders, we can take advantage of this process when we find ourselves in a place of anxiety or escalating emotion. Activating the curiosity tool allows us to re-enter into conversations with greater control over our emotions and with fuller thinking powers in place.

A second neurological benefit to triggering our inner curiosity is that our brain gets a boost of dopamine (the "feel good" neurotransmitter), which prepares our brain to receive and process new information more effectively (Matthias J. Gruber, 2014). Improved abilities to learn and take in data give us a competitive advantage and lead to better overall delivery outcomes from a "people" perspective, as well as an "outputs" perspective.

Now that we understand how curiosity can benefit you as a delivery leader, how do you leverage this tool?

The answer lies in cultivating curiosity in ourselves first, and then modeling and coaching this ability in our teams and the broader delivery context. We have curated our favorite hacks for developing and radiating personal curiosity:

CURIOSITY HACK #1: PRACTICE CURIOSITY

Our brains are drawn to pattern recognition. This leads to us having the ability to transfer skills and knowledge learned in one context to another, seemingly different situation. This means we can build our curiosity muscles by practicing in non-work situations. Embedding practices like actively pondering "What if" questions or thinking about our day-to-day activities and interactions in a different way will eventually train your brain to be more curious.

As a bonus activity, if you have the opportunity to observe children at play, you will notice that they approach life with a high degree of wonder and inquisitiveness. Join in the fun with them when possible. Interacting with and imitating their imaginative activities can give you a quick boost of curiosity.

CURIOSITY HACK #2: BREAKING BAD

We are often not aware of how our behavior, intentions and agendas affect our team and others around us. Our unconscious intentions and ways of behaving often create unintended outcomes, of which we are mostly unaware.

In his book *The Power of Habit* (Duhigg, 2012), Charles Duhigg talks about habit loops (these are neurological loops we create through repetitive, patterned behaviours), which can lead to negative outcomes. It looks like this:

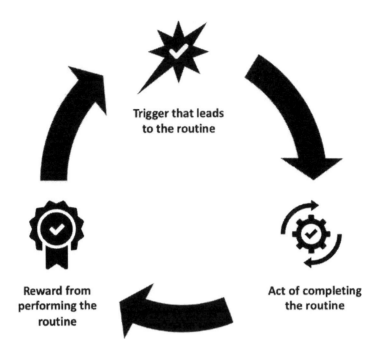

Trigger that leads to the routine

Act of completing the routine

Reward from performing the routine

How does this play out in real life? Has the following ever happened to you?

1. The team discusses an issue and everyone is talking. (Trigger: everyone talking)
2. You interrupt to get your word in. (Result: team thinks you must always get the last word)
3. The minute you get your word in, anxiety is released from the body. You feel better, but how does everyone else feel?

Are you truly listening to your team and actively looking for clues as to how you impact the team? How do you break out of this, or similar, bad habit loops?

Developing and heightening self-awareness abilities through channeling our inner curiosity can enable breaking the negative cycle by:

1. Enabling us to observe and become aware of our habit loop and its effect on others.

2. Recognizing that changing your behaviour will still result in a reward; this time it will be team satisfaction, rather than your individual satisfaction.

3. Training us to be patient. The ability to change your actions is impacted by how deeply ingrained the conscious or unconscious habit is (you know the saying: 'Old habits die hard').

If we really want to unlock the entire team's potential, we must recognize that both the cues and the rewards impact how we interact with others. It starts with you, and you cannot ask people to be curious without you demonstrating curiosity first.

CURIOSITY HACK #3: BE THE DIPLOMAT

As project managers, we often act as "diplomats" and mediate very difficult conversations. It is normal, when approaching these conversations that fear and anxiety bubble up to the surface. We tell ourselves stories about the situation: *"They are so difficult and want us to fail"* or *"They think I am not smart enough to lead this."*

When we go into conversations with these stories in our heads, we potentially sabotage our chances for a positive outcome.

Just as we can leverage curiosity to calm our inner demons in tough circumstances, as delivery leaders we can encourage our teams to enter into difficult conversations and situations with an attitude of curiosity. It will help them to control their emotions and eliminate unconscious bias (the stories we tell ourselves).

Intention Key.

This is not an exercise in getting back at people. If you always keep in mind that there are two sides to a story, remember to breathe deeply and flex your curiosity muscles, then the outcome can be powerful, because then you are truly open to all the opportunities. You become the learner when you create the right intentions!

Preparation

Ask yourself :
    a. What is my ideal outcome for this situation?
    b. What part of the conflict am I responsible for?
    c. Is there anything from my past that is being triggered here?

Be mindful about the time and place for the conversation

The Conversation

1. Your intent: Approach the person with curiosity, openness and a collaborative mindset
2. Be clear and use specific examples, avoid blaming language. Use language like: I notice and never used absolutes like "always" and "never"
3. Communicate from a place of feeling. "I felt__when you__. This was likely not your intention; however this was the impact on me.
4. Elicit the other person's perspective and listen without interrupting
5. Use silence with curious intent as a tool. Listen to the unspoken body language.
6. Own your own role in the conflict. When you said___I automatically stopped listening to you and became defensive, so I don't think I was totally open to what you were saying
7. If conversation gets heated set a boundary and ask to revisit with cooler heads

CURIOSITY HACK #4: ASKING QUESTIONS THE RIGHT WAY

As a leader, asking questions is part of our everyday responsibility. Asking them the right way elicits more powerful responses. For example, questioning assumptions embedded into costs and timelines can often be tricky. If we come at this from a state of curiosity rather than confrontation, we get better results. We can invite team members to put on their thinking caps to come up with other ideas when numbers do not cooperate. How creative can we get? Do not discard seemingly wild ideas right away; instead, open your mind and heart to the broadest possible options before focusing on a solution.

One caution: some managers attempt to inject "pseudo" curiosity by framing what is essentially an attacking statement in the form of a question. For example, asking in an aggressive tone or manner: *"I am curious why you did the plan this way instead of the way I suggested."* Your team member will likely detect the criticism and react defensively. Therefore, we advise that you never inject fake curiosity into your questions, bring instead a tone and body language that conveys genuine interest.

If you or your team becomes too heated, we suggest invoking the power of "mindfulness." Lena Ross, in her book *Hacking for Agile Change* (Ross, 2017, pp. 66-67), and Hamilton (Hamilton, 2015) both advise this practice that focuses on the "now" and being "present" in our interactions. The effort required to do this grounds us, mentally, while dampening the negative emotional thoughts that accompany difficult situations. When we do this, we create an environment that invites empathic listening and questioning and sets us up for a successful outcome.

SPREADING THE SEEDS OF CURIOSITY

We leave you with some final thoughts. Curiosity can become a way of being - enhancing the way we deliver projects. Unlocking the group's power of curiosity amplifies that magic further. Everyone can put his or her agenda aside, feel safe to have a transparent conversation about agendas and engage in open, innovative conversations that challenge assumptions and improve delivery.

So, why not bust out your inner child? Do something different, and ...

Live curiously and prosper!

SARAH RAMKISSOON AND KRISTINA RIIS

Together, Kristina Riis and Sarah Ramkissoon have almost 40 years of experience in the Investment Industry, with a focus on planning, process engineering and project management. Both Sarah and Kris believe that successful delivery stems from everyone being in a place where they are empowered to bring their full selves to work. They strive to create that type of work environment for themselves and well as their teams.

Before co-founding Impact Culture Inc., Kris led Project Delivery and the Agile Centre for Excellence at Ontario Teachers' Pension Plan. Her work in high-performance culture development blends facilitated design-thinking, cognitive change management and agile methodology to help leaders and their teams to work purposefully as they create new value and possibilities for their organizations.

Kristina Riis
Co-Founder and Chief Culture Officer
Impact Culture Inc.
Toronto, Ontario, Canada
https://www.linkedin.com/inkristina-riis-959b83
kris@impactculture.com

Sarah has strong expertise in various forms of leading delivery from Traditional to Agile methods. She leads the Practice Management area at the Ontario Teachers' Pension Plan, an organization where she has spent more than eleven years in a senior delivery capacity. Previously, she worked as a Project Manager for a US software company. She is passionate about delivery, not only from a "what is delivered" perspective but also "how it is delivered," and her day-to-day interactions are informed by her cognitive neuroscience and psychology background.

Sarah C. Ramkissoon, PMP, CSM, CSPO, MSW, BSc.
Senior Manager, Practice Management
Ontario Teachers Pension Plan
Toronto, Ontario, Canada
https://www.linkedin.com/in/sarah-ramkissoon-5751863/
polgara1603@icloud.com

RETOOLING YOUR LEADERSHIP CAPABILITIES
Assessing and Building on Your Ability to Lead Teams (and Yourself)

FRANK P. SALADIS

L eadership can be found in any organization and at any level within an organization. Generally, we associate the word *leadership* with people who have vision, passion, ability to motivate, clearly evident and strong values, a commitment to the organization, and the ability to attract and sustain followers. These are all important but it seems that the most successful leaders are those who focus a portion of their time and energy on the improvement of skills that will keep them in top "leadership form."

The question is: What is "top leadership form?

Something to consider: Every year, according to research, about 400 books are written about the topic of leadership. This means that despite all of the knowledge that has been accumulated for decades, there is no standard or universal definition of leadership. Strong and successful leaders can be categorized by different traits, personalities, behaviors and tactics. Some people who are referred to as "great leaders" were actually completely devoid of the skills we generally refer to as "interpersonal."

In the profession of project management, there seems to be a strong preference among organizational leaders and decision makers to select / hire project managers who can effectively balance their managerial skills with the softer people skills. Leadership behaviors that many organizational leaders (especially those in Human Resource Management positions) observe include:

- Informing
- Directing
- Clarifying
- Persuading
- Collaborating
- Brainstorming / Envisioning
- Reflecting
- Observing
- Disciplining
- Resolving Conflict
- Praising / Recognizing

The question to ask is: "How much time am I spending exhibiting or acting with these behaviors?" Example: If your typical day involves a significant amount of time in the behaviors of clarifying, directing, and resolving conflict, you may be dealing with some communications issues and should assess why you are spending so much time displaying those behaviors. An assessment of your typical daily leadership behaviors assists in defining where you should be spending your time. The outcome of this assessment is to determine the "ideal" balance of leadership behaviors for you and your organization or team.

The project manager, by nature of the position assumes a leadership role upon acceptance of any project assignment. Most project managers will agree that their position can be complex and involve multiple roles and significant responsibility. In many cases the responsibility is not matched with the authority that is sometimes needed to accomplish certain goals. To meet this challenge the project manager, or project leader, must call upon a certain skill set to maneuver through the ever-changing project environment and the demands of a wide variety of stakeholders. Over time, and through many projects, the project manager gains experience and becomes more adept at dealing with the demands imposed by clients, sponsors, and other stakeholders. Experience is certainly important and has significant value but, it does take a lot of time, and sometimes, experiences are not always pleasant! Another item to consider is that, in many cases, years of experience do not actually result in expertise. (Performing the same work poorly over many years can be claimed by someone as having "experience"). What a hiring manager should be asking about is the outcomes and what changed or has been improved through the individual's performance. A key factor here is not the years of experience; it is much more about outcomes, contributions, and value adding results.

In today's changing business and project environment, which is affected by an uncertain economy, rapidly changing technology and leaner workforces, there just may not be enough time to learn through experience. One must continually adapt to the environment and focus on improving acquired skills and adding new skills to maintain an edge as a <u>world class leader</u>. This requires the project leader to become a **world class learner**.

WORLD CLASS LEARNER AND WORLD CLASS LEADER

Leaders must invest in a "pay it forward" mode of personal growth. In addition, it is also important for the project leader to take an interest and encourage the personal growth of their team members. The business environment continues to change and as it changes, the need to learn as a team and to learn faster becomes essential if the organization plans to sustain its competitive advantage.

Leaders must examine the current state of their personal knowledge, the organizational knowledge at their place of business, review lessons learned, examine what others refer to as "best practices," make changes as needed, and anticipate the future needs of the organization and its clients. Change requires leaders to analyze organizational capabilities and equip themselves and their teams with the tools necessary to meet the next set of critical success factors and key performance indicators. From a leadership perspective, today's environment requires leaders to adapt quickly, align the team through common values, purpose, and a clear set of objectives. Leaders must create a sense of great opportunity within their organizations to attract the best talent and establish a desire for the team to work together toward shared aspirations. Opportunities include the potential for increased market-share, new product development, expansion into new business areas and simply, organizational growth.

The skills required to reach organizational objectives by managing resources (that are thinly dispersed and assigned to multiple projects and operations) are becoming increasingly important to obtain. Projects are becoming more and more complex and go well beyond the managerial skills we are most familiar with. There is certainly a need for planning, delegating, organizing, estimating, and other skills we associate with management, but today there is a much greater emphasis on skills that will improve personal time management, productivity, the ability to influence others, the ability to break down barriers and remove conflicts, and to motivate teams to go that "one step further." It is also important to have the ability to show sincere appreciation for work well done, to know when the pressures on the team begin to take their toll and when to provide a lighter, although probably brief, moment or two of rest, with, hopefully, some fun included. Skillfully providing praise or criticism is another area where many project leaders could use some further development

Consider your skills in the following areas:

- Setting team and individual goals – clearly stating meaningful objectives.
- Facilitating problem solving sessions.
- Communicating bad news.
- Delivering meaningful performance appraisals.
- Matching assignments with competency and talent.
- Setting clear expectations.
- Listening to others (really listening).
- Sincerely recognizing and acknowledging outstanding work.
- Creating a trusting environment that results in loyalty and commitment.

These are a few of the skills that many leaders possess, that could use some regular "sharpening." It is also important to anticipate new skills that will be required to remain effective. Virtual teams are common in business today and they require leaders who have the ability to create a strong connection among the team members regardless of time zone, customs, language, and values.

Revisiting the subject of "The World Class Learner," here are a few tips I learned from listening to a Keynote presentation by a well-known professional basketball player and business entrepreneur, Magic Johnson:

1. Be there first – be ready before others arrive.
2. Attitude – I'm here to win, Not really interested in 2nd place.
3. Go to the next level – go for the championship. Set your goals high.
4. Play against someone better than you. This is how you build skills.
5. Do a personal SWOT – Strengths, Weaknesses, Opportunities, and Threats.
6. Network – connect with lots of professionals.
7. Understand your customer – Really get to know them and their unspoken expectations.
8. Put your ego aside.
9. Uplift your Brand – Do not be "satisfied." Always focus in improving your reputation.
10. Give back – There are many personal rewards when your share.
11. Be demanding but fair – no clock watchers.
12. Know your team – stay connected and talk to your team often, especially virtual teams.

Retooling your leadership skills begins with a self- evaluation. Take the time to conduct a personal inventory of your skill sets. What are your strengths? In which skills do you feel you possess the greatest level of proficiency? Where is improvement needed? What will you be required to learn to stay at the same level and to advance, preferably, ahead of your competitors? How motivated is your team? How motivated are you? Are you displaying true enthusiasm for your project? Obtain some feedback from a trusted peer or arrange for a 3600 feedback or performance review. Taking a close look at where you are now, what you have accomplished, what you will need going forward and what your team needs to meet tomorrow's challenges will keep your skill set fresh, sharpened, and ready. The desire to retool, enhance skills and to stay in a continuous learning mode is a key success factor for the project leader, or any one in a leadership position, and paves the way to extraordinary leadership. Make it a point to develop your own criteria for your personal "Top Leadership Form" workout and then execute the plan with consistency and determination to reach your goal.

FRANK P. SALADIS

Frank P. Saladis, PMP, PMI Fellow is a Consultant, Instructor, a motivational speaker and an author within the discipline of project management. He holds a Masters Certificate in Commercial Project Management from GWU and is a graduate of the Project Management Institute Leadership Masters Class. He has held several positions within PMI including President of the NYC Chapter, President of the Assembly of Chapter Presidents and Chair of the Education and Training SIG. He is the author of 12 published books and is the originator of International Project Management Day. Mr. Saladis was recognized as PMI Person of the Year in 2006, PMI Fellow in 2013 and received the PMI Distinguished Contribution Award in October 2015.

AUTHENTICITY AS THE ART OF SUCCESS

TORY SALISBURY

I have found that the single most important technique during my project management career is being authentic. Why? People are drawn to it and it makes you more approachable, which in turn makes it easier to build and sustain relationships.

Then what does it mean to be authentic? If we think of buying a work of art which we believe is authentic, we believe it is genuine, real and we trust it has value. Experience will tell me that the real value we add to our tool kit is the ability to understand the impact we have on others. It is about how other's see us – how we communicate, what leadership style we use and how we engrain a sense of commitment and trust into our daily interactions. When leaders are rooted in authenticity, it creates enormous benefits for those they lead and for the organization overall.

Much of project management is about the "doing" and "getting things done" – i.e., the task-oriented nature of our jobs. What we do not have is a script or template for being authentic in what we do. It is often seen as an innate quality - you either have it or you do not. In fact, the qualities associated with authenticity can be developed over time.

I recall a project manager, Jim, who became very disenchanted and quite unhappy of where he was in his career. As he moved up the corporate ladder to a senior leadership role, responsible for multi-million-dollar projects, he became incredibly serious, distant and overly strict in the eyes of his employees. Staff became robotic in their interactions with him and responded out of fear.

I asked him how this made him feel and his response was that he wanted to fit into the corporate culture. Instead, he merely conformed to others' expectations and lost his ability to be an effective leader. His lack of authenticity eroded his sense of well being and left him feeling disengaged from both his self and the workplace. The discord between who he was and the cardboard cut-out image he created to look good diminished his aliveness.

As part of his coaching plan, we worked on challenging his assumptions about what his role entailed. He realized he did not have much experience in leading people or using influence within and outside the organization. He began taking leadership training and investing in the use of various tools to help him understand his communication and influence styles. He had to get to know himself better, as well as spend time with his staff to get to know them better. He understood his reputation for authenticity needed to be earned and carefully managed. Two years went by and I received a phone call from Jim – it was like talking to a different person – calm, confident, and ever so present. He even had a sense of humour. His final words to me were "Above all else, to thy own self, be true."

What Jim was conveying is the need to maintain and trust your authentic self. Your true core will always provide you with the most power, insight, intuition, empathy, and overall leadership capabilities that others can see. These are the same principles I use as a practicing project manager and facilitator. The ability to connect, share experiences, promote knowledge and instill trust is paramount to providing a safe and collaborative working or learning environment.

The following are three core principles that are the foundation to creating the authenticity we need to manage and lead our teams:

1. BUILDING TRUST

Many project managers have shared their views on leaders who are untrustworthy, lack transparency and compassion. These leaders may be sympathetic, but they lack empathy.

Building trust is about being consistent, providing sound judgement in what we say and do (walk the talk) and showing empathy. Empathy is the ability of a leader to sense and respond to the feelings of others. It is much easier to focus on why the schedule is behind (business issue) than to delve into challenging team dynamics (humanistic issue). Often in the need to succeed at a business level, we fail at the real issue that drives commitment and humility from those we lead - they just do not trust their leader.

2. LISTENING

Ironically, listening contains the same letters as silent. Our team members want to be heard. My experience will also tell me that leaders who listen create a sense of trust and openness that most people desire. It is the difference between listening to respond, vs. listening to react. Instead of pretending to be fully listening while you are in fact thinking of something else, listen with intent by looking at the person you are interacting with and avoid the distractions of devices and other barriers. Being genuine has a sense of "silence" to it.

3. COMMIT TO EXCELLENCE RATHER THAN PERFECTION

People naturally gravitate towards leaders who display humility, who do not have issues about being wrong and admitting it to their team. All of us, in some form, are a work in progress. We do make mistakes. Managers should to be open to learning from others, asking for help in areas unfamiliar to them, and showing themselves as real human beings.

In our VUCA (volatile, uncertain, complex and ambiguous) world, we will meet those that can inhabit and inhibit our authenticity. The key is to develop the skills to recognize and confront this paradox, just as Jim did. Changing our behavior to meet the expectations of inauthentic leaders is draining and affects not only our psychological well being, but our physical being as well. When we show up for work as our true selves, we can better connect with team members, project stakeholders, and ultimately our family and friends. This in turn builds trust.

If you are interested in learning more about being authentic, I suggest the following website. You can also take a Wired for Authenticity Assessment. Have fun!

https://www.transformleaders.tv/assessments/

TORY SALISBURY

 Tory Salisbury has over 20 year's professional experience in project and process management as a Consultant, Coach, Facilitator and Project Manager.

Tory has managed and consulted to organizations in Canada, the United States and the United Kingdom in the technology, aviation, insurance, government, banking, telecommunications, manufacturing, energy and utility industries. She has assisted organizations in the design and set-up of their PMO's including methodology frameworks. Tory also conducts strategic planning sessions and process reviews for non-governmental organizations.

As a skilled Facilitator and speaker, Tory delivers a variety of project management, communication and leadership courses/workshops for corporate and academic clients. Her background also includes instructional systems design, customizing training solutions and developing core competency models for Project Managers.

Tory is certified as a Project Management Professional (PMP) and is member of the Project Management Institute (PMI).

torysalisbury@bell.net
https://www.linkedin.com/in/tory-salisbury-32a6343a

THE FOUR PIECES OF INFORMATION YOU NEED FOR A BULLETPROOF PROJECT CHARTER

KANE TOMLIN

INTRODUCTION

"So wait, they need the webstore live by when?!?!" - I asked incredulously.

At The Emmy awards, a customer volunteered to be the prototype client so that they could have a live webstore for the Emmy's," my boss (codenamed M) replied, "Well, the prototype was only going to cost them $25,000 since our company is funding the enterprise project, and the whole point of being a prototype is that when things go wrong, the customer is not relying on a hard go-live date."

As an enterprise-wide initiative, the total cost was well in excess of a single webstore; however, we first had to integrate it into our Enterprise Resource Planning (ERP) system and develop a platform to dynamically generate webstores from the ERP data.

"True," he said, "but you need to figure it out anyway."

"We are going to have to crash the schedule, work 20 hour days, I'm going to need to spend the next two months in Florida onsite with the developers, and it's going to cost a fortune!"

Leaving a Michigan winter for a few months to work in Florida was a sacrifice I was willing to make, I'm a team player after all.

"That's fine," M replied, "they said money was no object."

"Everyone says that but no one *means* it," I mumbled sardonically.

"Well, do the math and let them know what the cost will be," M said, ignoring my complaining.

"Me?!?! - I thought that is why you got paid the big bucks?" I definitely did not want to be a part of *that* conversation.

"That sounds an awful lot like a 'not my problem' kind of issue there Mr. Project Manager," M stated, signaling the end of this conversation. I hated it when he was right, which was often.

Admittedly, my bedside manner was not very good 20 years ago, but my boss at the time was an awesome leader who let me vent and we had a great working relationship (and are still friends to this day). So, after crunching the numbers I was going to experience the joy of telling a top television network company that their $25,000 webstore was going to cost them over $400,000 in order to go-live in two months. Luckily for me, even way back in 2001-2002 (ish, my recollection of the ordeal is not perfect all these years later) I had a pretty good handle on the key elements of a good project charter…or at least I hoped I did as I picked up the phone to dial the project sponsor and beg for an additional $375,000…

SUMMARY

As unique as every project (and project charter) can be, there is one technique that has proven universally vital to my project, portfolio, program, and PMO management career. That is the ability to gather four pieces of information for every charter that I have ever drafted, and the tenacity and tact required to ensure that I get it every time, since this data is non-negotiable in my opinion. These key components are the triple constraints of the project (schedule, budget, performance constraints) and a strategic decompilation of the business case. While this may seem to be an easy data gathering task, it is in fact the most difficult part of the project manager (PM) and project sponsor's relationship; after-all, the sponsor does not usually like limitations on their project, a justifiable desire even if it severely hampers the PM. The process is both vital to project success and is typically difficult to execute, and hence it is often overlooked by PMs. With an industry-wide project failure rate close to 50%, it is imperative that we embrace best practices that increase success regardless of the challenges we face.

WHAT ARE THE TRIPLE CONSTRAINTS?

The Project Management Institute (PMI) is a great resource for a PM's needs; however, I feel PMI has shortchanged the importance of the triple constraints in project management in recent years. Projects have limited resources, a limited schedule, and tangible deliverables that need to be met. The triple constraints also known as the iron-triangle, is a way of understanding, visualizing, and ultimately managing these limitations. The triple constraint concept originated during the Apollo Moon Program by NASA 50 years ago and does not show any signs of becoming outdated (Launius, 1994). The triple constraints include: the schedule constraint (you do not have infinite time), the budget constraint (you do not have an infinite budget), and the performance constraints (the project's output has to perform desired results).

The art of project management usually comes down to the ability to understand and manage these constraints in relation to each other. Nothing exists in a vacuum and project management is no different. These constraints are related to each other; a change in one will have an impact on the other two. From my time in the Army as a dive school student (who ultimately became a master diver) I had the joy of writing the *General Gas Law* about a billion times as part of our nightly homework, it states: "temperature, volume, and pressure affect a gas in such a way that a change in one factor must be balanced by corresponding change in one or both of the others." (1993) In project management, the concept of the triple constraints should become a general project management law, though my attempts to create one, spread it into common vernacular, and reap the riches and worldwide acclaim have so far been unsuccessful; this may be due to my aforementioned suboptimal bedside manner.

Figure 1 – The Triple Constraints aka The Iron-Triangle

IDENTIFY THE DRIVER

As indicated in the above image (Figure 1), it is impossible to have a project that is low-cost, fast, and good quality (meet all performance constraints), therefore trade-offs will be required. As the old saying goes, 'you can have it good, fast, and cheap, now pick two'. One of the PM's most important roles in the charter stage is to identify these constraints and then identify the driver, or the most important/least flexible constraint. The constraint that is the driver will guide the PM during execution when things go wrong, as they invariably will. Using the digital catalog project example from the introduction, it is safe to say the driver was the schedule constraint, which meant that additional cost and or reduced performance criteria would be an acceptable price to pay to maintain the scheduled go-live date.

The challenge for the PM is to identify the driver through various techniques and then (and here is the hard part) have the sponsor accept the project charter with the driver identified. The sponsor needs to approve the driver to ensure that they understand their commitment and risk acceptance of the project while understanding that the driver will most likely cause the other constraints to shift if the project meets difficulty. Sponsor communication and education (if needed) is key at this stage, any miscommunications will come back to haunt the PM. The sponsor's signature on a project charter with the driver identified helps mitigate this risk during project execution.

IDENTIFY THE WEAK CONSTRAINT

Conversely, the PM should also identify the weak constraint using the same skills and tools used to identify the driver. This helps the PM identify the most flexible constraint on the project, and helps select project execution techniques. For example, if the approved weak constraint is the performance criteria, in essence the sponsor is acknowledging that their schedule and budget is limited but they are willing to "satisfice," to accept an available option as satisfactory, on the project's deliverables, which may indicate the project is a candidate for agile execution. However, if the schedule is the weak constraint then a lower priority, internally staffed waterfall style project may be a better fit. The PM also needs to know which constraint is the most flexible, so they can adjust accordingly when issues arise.

Remember, the triple constraints are related, and a shift of any one constraint will cause a shift in the other two. The PM's commitment to successful project completion means the PM needs to balance these constraints while consistently pursuing the driver as the highest priority. The sponsor and the PM need to be on the same page in this regard or the project is likely to fail. It is better to have a longer, possibly awkward planning stage to arrive at these conclusions than to start a project without them. Everyone's circumstances differ, but I have long considered this data to be non-negotiable, which means I am willing (and communicate this to my sponsors) to walk away from a project if I cannot get consensus on these constraints.

DECOMPILE THE BUSINESS CASE

The final piece of data required for a bulletproof charter is a decompiled business case. Many seemingly good projects fail due to misalignment of the project with the organization's overall strategy. The reasons that this may occur are beyond the scope of this chapter, however, as PMs we only need to know that it does happen in order to avoid this trap. Decompiling the business case from the strategic vision of the organization can be thought of as either a top town process where the strategic vision informs each project or conversely, moving from the "means" - aka the project, towards the "ends" - the strategy, can also work and is thought of as a more bottom-up approach. The bottom-up approach is usually the easiest to use when working with the project team.

In either scenario, the key is that the project's business case needs to be directly linked to a specific element of the organization's strategy. One training exercise I teach to illustrate this concept is the "'in order to' progressive elaboration." Starting with the project, continue to ask "in order to?" until your team runs out of answers. So a project to create a webstore might start with "in order to sell our products online." Why do we want to sell online? "In order to increase revenue and decrease costs," in order to… "increase customer retention and satisfaction by offering more value than any other webstore" which aligns to our mission to "deliver the best customer service possible." This very simple example illustrates one of the techniques needed to ensure strategic alignment which further armors your charter against project failure.

CONCLUSION

…armed with a bulletproof project charter, my phone call went surprisingly well. The television network customer understood why the non-driver constraints had to shift to accommodate a crashed schedule and they were willing to spend the money it would require to meet their needs. A few minutes during the project charter creation (and the Sponsor's signature) smoothed the road that led me to project success. That webstore is still live to this day, which is about the best result anyone can ask for in the world of project management.

KANE TOMLIN

 Dr. Kane Tomlin is a Project Management Professional (PMP®), holds a BS in Management Information Systems, an MS in Homeland Security and Emergency Management, a Doctorate in Strategic Security, and postgraduate certificates in Leadership Development and Project Management. Kane is a former U.S. Army Master Diver with 27 months in combat, and deployments spanning the globe. Kane is currently working as a management consultant for the state of Florida. Kane has over 20 years of project management experience, most notably as the director of the Project Management Office for the Florida Department of Law Enforcement.

Kane is a Professor of Applied Cybersecurity at Tallahassee Community College and a Professor of National Security at Excelsior College. Kane has served on many boards including PMI Tallahassee's Board of Directors as the Vice President of Professional Development and on Excelsior College's Board of Trustees. Kane is a keynote speaker on organizational strategy and project management. Kane is also an author of various books and articles published by the U.S. Army War College, the University of Louisville, the U.S. Army Publishing Directorate, and the Project Management Institute.

Dr. Kane Tomlin, DSS, PMP

TEKSystems, an Allegis Group Company
Tallahassee, FL
https://www.linkedin.com/in/kanetomlin/
Email: kanetomlin@gmail.com

BETWEEN THE TASKS

CHRIS VANDERSLUIS

As project managers we spend so much time thinking about each project task. When we work on being more efficient we focus on how we estimate tasks on how we sequence them. We think of the resources we apply to each task and we see where we could work a little more effectively. But, how much time do we spend looking in between each task? If you look beyond just the activities themselves in your projects and consider the entire workday of your resources, you may be quite surprised at what is not ever displayed on your project's bar-chart.

DISCOVERING IN-BETWEEN TIME

For some project managers looking to improve efficiencies, project reports have shown discrepancies that might have been otherwise overlooked. In an "as-built" project report for example, there can be a big difference between the total time reported on the project durations by resources and the total calendar time. Built reports are often done in situations where a team uses project scheduling software to attempt to re-create a now-completed project in order to find ways to do similar projects better in the future. Such teams look at each element of a project so a big delta between the resource time and the calendar time it took to finish projects needs to get explained. During the natural course of a project we do not tend to pause for such explanations. "Overhead," we might say if asked. However, a team looking at an as-built schedule will want to see if the amount of "overtime" is reasonable. If not, it too needs to be broken down and explained.

Another way to discover in-between time is a corporate timesheet. Project-only timesheets might be deceptive. They would typically record only the time on each task yet a corporate timesheet that is used for project purposes will need to account for the entire day. If the same timesheet used for the project progress is the one used to record the employee's entire workday, then all time must be accounted for. This can also show up when employees record the exact time they start a task and finish a task. This might be more relevant in an industrial environment; the gap between finishing one task and starting the next becomes of great interest in this context.

CASE STUDIES OF IN-BETWEEN TIME

In our work deploying project and timesheet systems, we have partnered with a number of efficiency teams looking for how to improve project efficiency. The work spans many industries. Here are two examples:

MANUFACTURING

We had the chance to work with a manufacturing company in the Midwest USA where the project management office had been presented with a challenge by the corporate VP. The company was based in a mid-sized town where they were the dominant employer and where their decades-old business had expanded across the town into multiple buildings and facilities. Some offices were on the same campus, others were across town and to facilitate movement of staff, the company provided continuous shuttles between buildings.

The corporate VP had noticed a line of employees at the shuttle stop one morning and asked the project management office that day how much time the corporation spent on inter-office transport. No one had any idea.

Within a few days, the company's timesheet system had new tasks and the entire 1,200-person staff were advised that the "internal-transport/local" - "internal-transport/regional" and "internal-transport/out-of-state" had to be filled in whenever they applied. Ninety days later, the results were in. Over 15% of time was spent by project personnel on moving around from place to place. The cost of moving people around was millions of dollars and the opportunity cost of those people being transported instead of doing project work was significant.

The day after the report was released, corporate management issued two company-wide directives. First, all project personnel would be co-located to the maximum extent possible starting immediately. Next, if in-person meetings were required, the fewest number of people would transport. It turned out that many staff would often travel from their project location to where senior management was located in order to present a report. This new directive meant that senior management would have to go to the project offices. This soon resulted in fewer in-person meetings with the whole project staff having to wait at the bus stop. The impact of the implementation of these two changes was to reduce internal transport over the next year to a much more acceptable 4%.

MAINTENANCE SHUTDOWN PROJECTS

A number of years ago, I had the opportunity to work directly with a team in the steel industry. Their projects were shutdown, turn-around maintenance projects that would occur only two or three times a year and would take only six days or so to finish. This team was determined to find efficiencies in the process that had previously been undiscovered.

The incentive was large. For every extra hour a shutdown project goes on, the opportunity cost to the company is the steel they cannot produce. This can be hundreds of thousands of dollars an hour. The team found two areas that ultimately saved over 25 hours in each process. The first was transit time within the plant from one task to the next. For these workers, this meant shifting a team with tools supplies and equipment from one location to another within the plant.

No one had ever considered before the impact of moving from one side of the plant to the other, then moving right back again to where they started. The team added a distance factor for the link between each task and, as a result, was able to resequence many tasks to group those closer together in the schedule. The savings across hundreds of workers was massive.

The second big discovery was waiting time. Workers had been given tasks and assigned durations based on estimates that were over a decade old. It had been years since anyone had asked them how long each task should take. Instead, if a task was scheduled for example for six hours but only took two, the next team would not arrive until the original scheduled task. This resulted in teams just waiting until they could move to the next task.

The total savings resulted in millions of dollars per shutdown.

INTERRUPTIONS

The biggest in-between time savings of all may be associated to interruptions. Have you ever wondered how much time you are losing when someone says "have you got a minute?" According to University of California, Irvine researcher Gloria Mark, it takes an average of 23 minutes and 15 seconds to get back to your original task.[1]

In today's instant access world, that can be significant. We are all connected with mobile phones, chatting services, internet-connected watches and other technology. When we think of the benefits of using chat technology like Slack or Microsoft Teams, we usually think of how convenient it is for the requestor, not how disruptive it is for the requestee. Something that looks so attractive from a theoretical point of view like the pop-up notice that you have mail, can interrupt your thinking multiple times an hour.

If you use Ms. Mark's analysis, 20 interruptions a day means never getting anything done that you had originally planned.

In our own office we combat interruptions for technical staff with several techniques. First, we have disabled all email pop-ups, and it is requested that staff check their mail every couple of hours, not every couple of minutes.

Next, we have "no-chat" windows where technical staff turn off their instant chat technology for a couple of hours at a time and turn their

---

[1] https://www.ics.uci.edu/~gmark/chi08-mark.pdf

phone to do-not-disturb, in order to be able to concentrate on work they need to accomplish.

FINDING YOUR OWN BETWEEN THE TASKS TIME

Anyone who is now finding the notion of tracking time between the tasks can take action almost immediately. The examples of the many organizations we have worked with who have found such time and improved efficiency as a result have all come about through observation. Where is the time going? What do people do when they are not working on tasks? We do not encourage looking for how much time people spend on taking care of themselves. Cutting down on a few minutes of break time or how long someone is allowed to use the restroom is not effective. This kind of intrusion can cause massive heartache with staff relations. The types of in-between tasks you can be looking for are those which no one wants to do. No one likes interruption. No one likes waiting at a bus-stop in the middle of a busy day.

If you are not sure where to start, collecting the 'actuals' is a good place. First, if you do not have a task-based timesheet, think of implementing one. Next, think of adjusting your internal timesheet to ensure accounting for the whole day (not just task time). Finally, delving into your project database can reveal huge savings.

CHRIS VANDERSLUIS

Mr. Vandersluis is the president and founder of HMS Software based in Montreal, Canada. HMS was created in 1984 as a company specializing in Project Management and Time-sheet systems.

HMS started as a consulting and distribution firm deploying project systems in Canada and creating custom built add-ons to those systems such as timesheets. This brought HMS and Mr. Vandersluis to large Canadian clients in the utilities, manufacturing, aerospace and defense industries.

In 1994, Mr. Vandersluis transformed HMS into a project management software publishing firm with the launch of the TimeControl timesheet system. TimeControl is a project-based timesheet system known as one of the most flexible and integrateable timesheets in the world. It includes links with some of the largest project management systems including those from Microsoft, Oracle, Deltek EPM, Bright-Work and ARES PRISM. These technical alliances have brought Mr. Vandersluis into many of the firms you recognize for project management today.

Mr. Vandersluis has been published in numerous publications including Fortune Magazine, Heavy Construction News, the AMA Handbook on Project Management and the Ivey Business Journal. He has written columns for PMI's PMNetwork magazine, Computing Canada magazine, Microsoft's TechNet and Project Times and is the author of the popular project management blog EPMGuidance.com.

He has taught Advanced Project Management at Montreal's McGill University and speaks at project management association functions across North America and around the world.

Mr. Vandersluis has been a member of PMI since 1986.
Chris Vandersluis
President, HMS Software
Montreal, QC
https://www.linkedin.com/in/cvandersluis/
chris.vandersluis@hms.ca
514-695-8122 x223

PUTTING CUSTOMER EXPERIENCE AT THE HEART OF PROJECT DELIVERY

JARETT HAILES

Successfully delivering a project depends on many factors: team talent, sponsor leadership, technical expertise, and the ability to manage challenges that pop up out of nowhere. The project management profession has matured over the decades to help teams deliver on time, on budget, in scope, and with a sufficient level of quality.

Nonetheless, is it enough? Despite all our advances in project management over the years, delivery is often still challenged. Even when projects end up meeting their targets, the people working on the project may not feel like it was worth it. Over the years, I have seen and been involved in projects that hit all their milestones, and on paper, they were a success; yet, you would never want to go back and work on those projects again.

To improve the chances of meeting successful outcomes, there is an important concept from modern design theory we can leverage. I have found this concept not only makes it more likely you will achieve your goals; it also makes the process of going through a project more enjoyable for all involved.

Customer experience is defined as the interactions a person has with your organization and the resulting perceptions they have. While indirect interactions (such as marketing) play a part in their perceptions, the strongest impressions are usually left when dealing directly with your company as they search out, receive, and use a good or service.

APPLYING CUSTOMER EXPERIENCE PRINCIPLES TO PROJECTS

Customer experience practices have predominantly been associated with product and service delivery. Mega-successful companies such as Amazon and Ritz-Carlton have made the customer experience their top priority in everything they do. A cottage industry of accreditation services has popped up to help people demonstrate their talent with delivering positive customer experiences, as more companies want to improve how they are perceived by their current and potential customers.

If you are working on a project, you can apply customer experience principles in two ways:

- Consider the end customer of the product or service being developed by your project and how they will interact with the offering once the project is complete; and
- Treat project stakeholders as customers and develop an in-project customer experience to maximize the chances of success.

In this chapter, I will focus on how you can embed a great customer experience into your projects. As a project manager you can lead the work I will be describing. However, your team needs to be involved to get the most diverse perspectives and deepest insights in order to deliver a better customer experience.

DEFINING YOUR CUSTOMERS

Let us start with defining customers from a project perspective. Here is a list of the people I typically treat as my key customers on a project. You can add or remove people or groups as needed:

- Project sponsor;
- Steering committee;
- Subject matter experts who are not part of the project team but provide input;
- End customers of the product or service being developed; and
- Operations team members who will support the product or service once it is ready to be deployed.

Each of these individuals or groups represents a different type of customer. They have different needs, expectations, and goals for the project, and interact with the project and its team differently.

For each customer, we want to start with understanding what value they are getting out of the project:

	Customer	Value of Project to Customer
	Project Sponsor	Unit's productivity expected to increase 20%. Meet regulatory requirements – avoids fines of $500K, annually
	Steering Committee	Performance bonuses dependent on project success
	Subject Matter Experts	None – being told they must participate
	End Customers	Reduced time on menial tasks
	Operations Team	Increased bonuses after shifting time to revenue generating activities Less work to maintain new solution compared to current state.

Not every stakeholder will necessarily receive value out of a project – it is important to identify this so we can plan to engage those people accordingly, as they are not incentivized to participate.

After we identify customer groups, we want to come up with a persona that represents the typical person in that group. If the group has highly varied makeup of people, we may want to make several personas. Personas help us identify some of the key traits that will drive the perceptions and behavior of the individuals in the customer group.

Let us focus on the operations team. We will create a persona for the team that identifies the key relevant traits of the team members to help us build a great customer experience.

Nancy: Operations Team Specialist	
 **Years Experience: 3** **Years with Company: 1**	**Key Traits** • Supports 70 different products and services • Receives 5 requests for change on supported offerings daily • Frustrated at getting poor support documentation when projects complete • Hasn't been asked to provide input into solution design • Will likely leave operations team in next 12 months for another department or company

Based on our persona and value assessment, next we develop an **empathy map**. Empathy maps allow us to 'get in the head' of our personas and help us to understand how they perceive the project and the problem it is trying to solve. Empathy maps capture:

- What the customer sees and hears with respect to our project (from the project team or others).
- What they think and feel about the project.
- What they say and do while interacting with the project.
- What are the pains and gains they may experience when interacting with the project.

Below is a simple empathy map for Nancy:

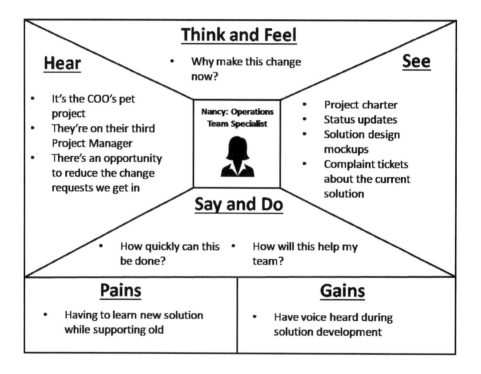

DEVELOPING THE CUSTOMER JOURNEY

Once we have a good sense of our customers and what matters to them in the context of our project, we can develop a **journey map**. Journey maps are used to model how someone interacts with the project. Unlike process diagrams, they do not worry about how something works, but instead focus on what occurs and what the results of that interaction are.

To set up the journey, we scope it to achieve a particular end goal. For projects, I usually select something related to the completion of the project; however, depending on the customer, it may make sense to pick a different end point such as completion of a critical milestone.

Journey maps can be created for the current state describing how your customers experience the project or a target future state. I usually build out a current state journey map first, as that will give us an opportunity to look for opportunities to make their experience with our project better. At each interaction point along the journey, we want to estimate how positive or negative that experience is for our customer, what factors could affect that experience (in terms of potential breakdowns in customer service), and how we could improve our interactions with that customer.

Here is a simplified journey map for Nancy from when she first hears about the project to when her team is handed over the product from the project team:

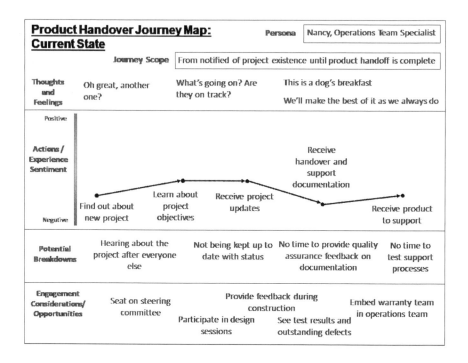

Product Handover Journey Map: Current State

Persona: Nancy, Operations Team Specialist

Journey Scope: From notified of project existence until product handoff is complete

Thoughts and Feelings	Oh great, another one?	What's going on? Are they on track?	This is a dog's breakfast. We'll make the best of it as we always do	
Actions / Experience Sentiment (Positive — Negative)	Find out about new project	Learn about project objectives · Receive project updates	Receive handover and support documentation	Receive product to support
Potential Breakdowns	Hearing about the project after everyone else	Not being kept up to date with status	No time to provide quality assurance feedback on documentation	No time to test support processes
Engagement Considerations/ Opportunities	Seat on steering committee	Provide feedback during construction · Participate in design sessions	See test results and outstanding defects	Embed warranty team in operations team

Using a journey map is a great way to take ourselves out of our own viewpoint of the project and look at it from someone else's perspective. We may think we have good project management and delivery practices in place, but it is how others perceive those outputs that matter.

Once we have looked at how things work today, we can set a target future state journey. In our example with Nancy, we see how disconnected her team feels from the project, as they are not engaged much at the beginning or during the project. However, at the end of the project they are expected to be able to run with the project's output and make it an ongoing success.

With this insight, we can look for ways to get Nancy's team more engaged up front and throughout the project. Here is a future state journey map that adds new interactions and improves the experience during existing interactions. We also identify measures that will help us ensure we are on the right track with the team as we progress through the project:

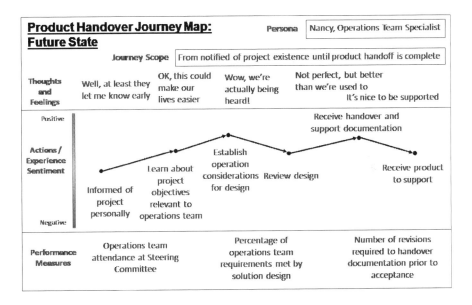

Once we have developed target journeys for our key customers, the project team reviews how we are currently or were planning on running the project and implements the changes necessary to make certain our customers have a positive experience throughout the journey.

DRIVING SUCCESSFUL OUTCOMES THROUGH CUSTOMER EXPERIENCE

Why spend all this time on making your project stakeholders happy with the project implementation? Are the project outcomes all that should matter?

In my experience when project stakeholders feel like they are being well taken care of, they are willing to go the extra mile for your project when it needs it. Projects never run completely smoothly; by providing a great customer experience for your stakeholders, you are increasing their loyalty to you and your team.

Maybe there is a tight deadline that requires some overtime from your subject matter experts, or your team missed a critical requirement and the operations team needs to develop workarounds at the last minute. By giving your stakeholders the best experience possible, they are willing to work with you when things get tough.

By making the customer experience a central component of how you manage and deliver projects, you will find that you not only achieve better outcomes at the end of the project, but you and your stakeholders will have a more enjoyable experience working on the project as well.

JARETT HAILES

Jarett Hailes is President of Larimar Consulting Inc. Since 2007, he has worked with organizations to deliver solutions with happier internal and external customers throughout the process. Jarett typically works on large-scale eight and nine figure transformations that span multiple organizations and stakeholder groups. Prior to consulting, Jarett co-founded two start-up companies out of university, commercializing mathematical intellectual property by applying it to the financial and targeted advertising industries.

Jarett is the author of Business Analysis Based on BABOK® Guide Version 2 – A Pocket Guide, which was written to help people understand the value of business analysis and how to get the most out of the Business Analysis Body of Knowledge. Jarett also teaches at the University of Alberta and MacEwan University and enjoys learning from students as much as they learn from him.

To connect with Jarett, you can reach out to him on LinkedIn at https://www.linkedin.com/in/jaretthailes.

SUCCESSFUL PROJECT MANAGERS SERVE THEIR TEAM'S THREE BASIC NEEDS

DAVID BARRETT

I took over a project recently that had all the markings of a great success. And then, I met the people inside that project. They are upset, miserable and most importantly, confused. My predecessor, it seems, had made the popular mistake of worrying only about project completion – and not project success.

In my mind, project success is certainly about completion, but success also has a people component and I would suggest that three key questions will help you understand if you were paying attention to real project success.

I call these the 'Project Team Member's three basic needs'.

1. They want to be happy and heathy during and after project completion.
2. They felt well informed during the lifecycle of the project. They knew what they needed to know at the right time and in the right format.
3. They felt 'under control' during the project.

When I address project teams and audiences about successfully managing people within a project environment, I like to suggest that their ultimate goal should be to be a 'desired project manager'. When they select the project manager for the next gig, you want to be the one that everyone wants to work for. Believe me, as successful as you might be, it is not your track record they are looking at. They care about themselves first and their three basic needs:

1. TO BE HAPPY AND HEALTHY

What does this mean? It means your people like coming into work every day. It is fun. They feel that management, and you, care about them and their personal well-being. They are meeting new people and growing their contact base along the way. They are challenged on a regular basis – pushed to be better and to learn new skills. They are connected to the business needs – the 'why we are doing all of this' which makes the job that much more interesting. And, they are growing professionally - learning on the job, and being encouraged to move forward. Furthermore, they are quickly moving up in the organization and even in the industry.

Making all this reality is tall order. My first suggestion is that we cannot do all of these yourself. Seek help from others. If you are light in one of these areas, get some training or coaching in areas you are not as strong at. If you are not a good motivator – take a course on employee motivation. If you are not as empathetic as you might want to be – get someone else to help you fill this gap.

But, regardless of whether you, or someone else delivers to the need, pay attention. The leader who is eyes open among his or her employees will win the much-desired respect at the end of the day.

Paying attention means connecting to your team in any way possible. Consider an 'office walk-about' every week or so. Find time to spend one-on-one with team members to get to know them. This will go a long way. Many employees will say that they felt more important than just an employee - to their manager, and this was a major reason for their loyalty to the company.

Many organizations are still asking for the annual employee review or job performance review. This is too bad. Regardless of the organization's requirements, do this more often than once a year and do it as informally as you want. In today's environment, a year can be a long time. If appropriate, shorten this time span and check in with your employees more often.

2. TO BE WELL INFORMED

Your project team members want to know what is going on – and how it relates to them. They have work to do for you and they want to do it well. It is your responsibility to get them the data or information they need at the right time, in the right format. Keeping them abreast of project progress, changes, critical issues (that relate specifically to them) and more, is essential in the delivery of the second basic need. No one wants surprises. It is your job to avoid them – by keeping everyone well informed.

How can you make this happen? The first thing I would suggest is to be sure you spend time upfront in all your projects on the stakeholder identification and a communications plan. Too often, we are making major assumptions about 'who's who in the zoo' and getting into a lot of trouble as a result.

The stakeholder analysis should help you identify everyone who can 'make or break your project any time in the life-cycle of the project' as they say. This time spent will help you understand who the key players are and who the people are who think they are key players, but are not.

The communications plan will grow out of the stakeholder analysis. It helps us understand who gets what, why, where, and when. It identifies key data flow both in and out of your project and connects that data to the people who should get it.

These two important tools and the steps creating them will never ensure everyone is kept informed, but it will come pretty close.

Once you have identified the stakeholders within your project and who gets what, why and when – you can deal with the 'how' part of keeping them well informed. We have many tools available to us as project leaders that can be used to transfer information ranging from status reports, regular meetings, email, texts and even the phone. My words of wisdom when it comes to deciding on the tool to use is that one size does not fit all and scalability is critical. Are your team meetings too large or too long – scale them down. Are your reports too long –shorten them. Are your presentations too detailed, scale them back.

Look at your audience and ask yourself, if you were in that audience, how would you like to see the information presented? How long should it take? What format would be appropriate? And even... are you in the right venue to get the message across effectively?

Your audience is not all the same and one size certainly does not fit all. Split up your audiences as required. Deliver short and precise information to the leadership team and keep the details for the troops. Your success relies on your ability to read your audiences well before you communicate with them so that the message lands well.

3. TO BE UNDER CONTROL

While similar to #2 above, this is quite different. This is not so much that he, or she, is under control, but it goes to the feeling that the whole project is under control. No one wants to work for a sinking project or a project that is running out of control and destined to disaster.

This basic need is a comfort thing, a feeling of security that all is well with the world – or at least, the project world in which we are working.

This one certainly involves a good level of communication throughout the project. However, this communication flow involves more than just project data to help resources get their work done. This flow of information includes the news and updates as to how we are doing as a team. How the next few months look and how we are doing on our commitments to our stakeholders. Our team members want to be a part of this conversation. As a team member's basic need, it delivers to the feeling of security and well being.

How can I make this happen?

Learn how to communicate well – to everyone. Learn about the importance of connecting the end results to the current day status – being sure people always (or almost always) know where they are headed, where they are today and what it will take to get from here to there. Hold meetings that address the big picture and not just the detailed project stuff. Establish and publish or announce major mile-stones and bring everyone in on the action. Celebrate small wins as you reach every milestone instead of waiting.

Good communications skills will help immensely in this area. Learn how to communicate well and you will be fine.

Project success is much more than just on time and on budget. It is about all of that and the health, safety, and happiness of every single one of your team members. You cannot afford to lose any of them – so do not.

DAVID BARRETT

 David Barrett is a professional speaker, regular blogger, podcast host, author, co-author or co-complier of five books, education advisor and co-compiler of this book.

These days he specializes in speaking and facilitating workshops in the area of strategy execution for all audiences.

David is the founder and National Program Director for the Centre of Excellence in Project Management at The Schulich Executive Education Centre, Schulich School of Business, York University.

He was the founder and Managing Director of ProjectWorld Canada and Project Summit USA and the founder and Executive Editor of ProjectTimes.com.

David has also created a new project management event called ProjectTalks.

TEAM BELLYFIRE

CANDICE DAVIS

WHAT IS BELLYFIRE?

It should be no secret that project teams deliver results, not processes. There is a plethora of techniques, processes and templates that can be used to manage projects. Layer all the execution methodology options on top of that and there is an exorbitant selection of tools to support project execution. The application of these tools is a combination of art, science, and life experience. What if there was one more thing you could add to the execution equation that provided for less of that. Imagine projects executed with more passion than process. Imagine project teams brought together with the commonality of overwhelming drive and determination. Imagine project teams powered by a subtle energy that creates a momentum upsurge. Let us call it the success multiplier. Let us call it Bellyfire.

Got Bellyfire? We all do - we just may not call it that. Bellyfire, (a.k.a. passion) powers so much of what excites, engages and drives us. Bellyfire is the fuel that ignites and charges us in achieving our goals, facing our fears and following our heart. People who show up with passion and a sense of purpose on a project team become a significant contributor to amplifying project success. A project team that is totally powered by Bellyfire stands out in a crowd, or organization, and has a success factor that creates curiosity and awe.

How do you create Team Bellyfire? You recruit Bellyfire. You foster Bellyfire. Recruiting a project team, and fostering a project environment that has Bellyfire, takes time, open and honest conversation, and listening to your gut! It does not happen accidently; it happens by design.

RECOGNIZING BELLYFIRE

Someone with Bellyfire has positive energy, exudes passion for high quality work product, is willing to go the extra mile to deliver 'wow factor', is known to be a person of integrity, does what they say they are going to do, and is a transparent communicator. In addition, their personal acumen is punctuated with:

- team focus,
- compassion,
- eagerness to learn,
- active listening,
- self motivation,
- ability to see things through, and
- acknowledgement of areas where they can develop.

When you have a team of people that share any number of these attributes, you need less process and have more trust. Team members are self motivated to achieve the end goal, persevere together, and feel accountable to the team, ultimately, naturally, and willingly supporting each other to final success.

RECRUTING BELLYFIRE

A regimented recruiting-by-design strategy is key. When recruiting Bellyfire there are attributes that will ensure individuals have what you want. Here are eight (8) things to consider when recruiting Bellyfire.

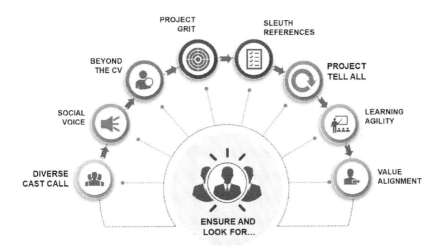

RECRUITING BELLYFIRE

DIVERSE CAST CALL

Often, recruitment starts by looking for someone who has done the exact role that is looking to be filled. In another words, if a role is for a software development senior project manager in a certain industry then a role description and recruitment strategy is tailored to look for someone who has done that exact role. The challenge with this approach is that diversity is stifled from the start. Looking for resources that come from different industries with similar skill sets may not come through normal recruiting channels. It is incredible what talent can be found when you cast the net far and wide.

SOCIAL VOICE

Everyone has a personal brand and one of the ways you define a brand is through your social voice. More and more candidates have a social media presence and a distinct voice on those channels. If a resource is active on social media, it is important to confirm the things they are talking about align with what they are sharing in an interview.

BEYOND THE CV

The curriculum vitae (CV) is a starting point. CV's outline accomplishments that tend to be tailored to the role that is being recruited. We have all been trained to 'tailor our resume' for the role by using buzz words, highlighting similar experience and framing ourselves in a mirror image of the advertised role.

One common trait people with Bellyfire have is a desire to step it up and look for opportunities to do more than they have done in their last role and that means applying for roles that they may not have the experience for. It is important to learn more about a candidate than what is on the CV. The personality of the candidate is not normally well depicted on paper and getting to know the personality is what confirms the presence of Bellyfire.

PROJECT GRIT

Executing projects is tough work and delivering successful projects is even more so. Not everyone is cut out for or likes tough work; however, someone who can be identified as having 'staying power' is evidence of grit. Grit is really a combination of passion and perseverance that brings something across the finish line. No one remembers the easy projects, nor do they describe them as the most rewarding. When interviewing candidates, bring the challenging projects into the picture and understand how they handled and contributed to taking them across the finish line.

SLEUTH REFERENCES

Candidate provided references present minimal consolation in a hiring decision. Candidate provided references tend not to be the ones that you really want.

Perform some reference work yourself. Talk to people in your network who may know the candidate or cold call people in the candidate's network. It is amazing how different the interview process goes when you start with information or insights you realized from searching out your own information. Let the interview validate things you have heard. Not the other way around. You want to have heard something that makes you excited to meet the person.

PROJECT TELL ALL

Disclosing the current or anticipated challenges in a project is vital. A candidate that understands potential challenges walks in with eyes wide open; shock value is reduced or eliminated. So, if a candidate is up for cited challenges, that exhibits a lot about their personality.

LEARNING AGILITY

The willingness to learn from experience and then apply that learning in a project environment is evidence of learning agility. Hiring project team resources that do not know it all is healthy. The learning gap provides an opportunity for growth and support from other resources. It allows project resources to gather new information and seek out experiences that have the potential to greatly improve results.

VALUE ALIGNMENT

Alignment between personal/career and company/project core values is essential. Alignment is key to creating satisfaction, a sense of fulfilment and happiness that inspires people to do their best work. When you have team members that share the same values they work better together, there is less conflict, they feel more dedicated - to not only show up but perform within the team - with increased productivity, accountability and commitment. When values are aligned there is inner motivation that fuels a drive to complete a task because you know the contribution has a positive impact on project success.

FOSTERING TEAM BELLYFIRE

A valuable activity to foster Team Bellyfire is working together to create a team résumé. The résumé is best made up of six things: strengths, weaknesses, fears/doubts, learning opportunities, passions, and résumé adders.

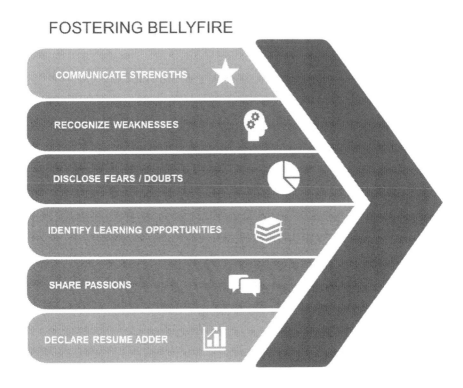

FOSTERING BELLYFIRE

- COMMUNICATE STRENGTHS
- RECOGNIZE WEAKNESSES
- DISCLOSE FEARS / DOUBTS
- IDENTIFY LEARNING OPPORTUNITIES
- SHARE PASSIONS
- DECLARE RESUME ADDER

Communicate Strengths / Recognize Weaknesses: Knowing each individual team members' strengths and weaknesses is powerful. It is amazing what talents people have that we do not know about and that can be translated into value in a project environment.

Disclose Fears/Doubts: Sharing fears and doubts is something that should be an encouraged activity. Once team members have shared those feelings, they are no longer a distraction.

Identify Learning Opportunities: There is gratification, excitement and a sense of accomplishment that we experience when we have learned something new. Showing up on a project team and declaring that you may not know something (but would like to learn it) is not a normal occurrence. When we identify knowledge vacancies it is amazing to see how other team members step up and teach.

Share Passions: Everyone is passionate about something and you need to get to know individuals and ask some questions to figure out what those things are. Like having conversations about strengths and weaknesses; it is important to have a passion conversation so they can be cultivated in the project.

Declare Résumé Adder: Adding a project success to one's résumé is an ideal goal, but the accomplishment of that success is a result of team endeavor. Sharing a résumé adder that each team member would like to compliment their résumé is an important exercise.

FUEL THE FIRE

Building a team fueled by Bellyfire is a conscious decision that takes time, commitment, and conversation with leadership. It is about honoring first impressions, trusting your gut and being energized and excited after you meet someone. Although it may happen accidently sometimes, the correlation to project success is multiplied when Bellyfire is consciously recruited and fostered. Once you have been part of a team fueled by Bellyfire you will never want to be part of one that is not. Seek Team Bellyfire!

CANDICE DAVIS

Candice Davis is described as high-energy, entrepreneurial spirited and passionate about project management, strategy and change management. Ms. Davis has held various project management leadership roles in the legal, construction and oil and gas industries. Over the last two decades, Candice has created and led several Project Management Offices, Programs and Portfolios. Candice is currently a management consultant with The Censeo Group.

Ms. Davis currently teaches project management at Mount Royal University (MRU) and the Southern Alberta Institute of Technology. In addition to teaching at MRU, Candice has led the curriculum development of two new project management certificates: Applied Project Management and Construction Project Management. She has chaired the MRU Project Management Advisory Committee and was an Advisory Committee member at the University of Alberta, School of Business, and Executive Education.

She completed her Bachelor of Management degree from the University of Lethbridge. Candice is also a graduate from Stanford University in Strategic Decision Analysis and Risk Management. Ms. Davis holds her Project Management Professional designation as well as a Change Management Certification. She is also a graduate from the Canadian Board Diversity Council Program.

Candice received her Fellowship from the Project Management Institute and received a Distinguished Teaching Award from MRU. She was named a Top 100 Protégée in Canada's Women's Top 100 Most Powerful Mentoring Program by the Women's Executive Network twice. Candice is currently on the Leadership Council for the Forward Summit.

Candice's shows up with Bellyfire!

Contact Candice at 403.680.8841 or candice@bellyfire.com.

THE STAKEHOLDER REGISTER
A Map for Traversing the People of your Project

AZIZ DURANAI

OPPORTUNITY

*T*he Stakeholder Register serves as a 'Master Key' in enabling one to understand, define and achieve any aspect of the project. Its inherent nature gives way to assembling the characteristics of the projects life forces – for it is the living people who think and do, and who make the decisions to construct something useable of value out of nothing and parts while using the power of imagination to innovate and create. As the simplest yet arguably most effective tool amidst the myriad of project management tools, I strive to keep it in my back pocket because it enables my team to stay united and keeps my clients close.

The Stakeholder Register has been helpful to me in many project scenarios throughout my decade-plus tenure in the network technology infrastructure domain. Just as how network technology infrastructure has become the digital veins of organizations, I view the Stakeholder Register as the veins of projects – interconnecting the people and parties involved and affected. I am grateful for the experiences this unique playground has made available to me – wearing different hats and serving in varying capacities while being exposed to many departments, technologies, processes, systems, problems, vendors, and of course, people. It is a world where technology, capabilities and roles consistently evolve, and where change is always high in volume – all underlined with a need for exact precision, given that a slight configuration error can cause dire business-impacting consequences. This environment has prompted my observation of projects being a 'way of life' as if to be a minimum standard in organizations. The atmospheres of organizations are becoming increasingly common for continuously running projects that are large in number and size, with a need to deliver and control them with minimal defects in a fast-paced fashion on hard-set deadlines. It, therefore, becomes essential to run projects optimally by using the tools and techniques that will bring forth value without introducing unnecessary administrative overhead. This is what makes the practice of project management both an art and a science.

The Stakeholder Register has been especially helpful to me in enforcing a sort of 'Unity' in untraditional **Wicked Projects**[2] – a non-formulaic breed of projects that affects many individuals and teams, where the meat of efforts requires a heavy focus on designing the solution before subsequent execution efforts can be identified. The complex and unfamiliar nature of these cross-functional projects generally presents challenges in delays, conflicting views and issues in securing and effectively utilizing dedicated project resources and funds. Much of these difficulties arise when attempting to attain alignment across affected departmental towers. It is a generally accepted fact that an increase in the number of affected parties in a project correlates to an

---

[2] *The term 'Wicked Project' mentioned above is an offshoot of the term 'Wicked Problem' first coined and raised popularity by Horst W.J. Rittell and Melvin M. Webber in their 1973 published paper 'Dilemmas in a General Theory of Planning'*

increase in communication channels and authorized approvers. As such, it is more than likely that an organization's established departmental structures and project management pipelines may not be positioned to optimally manage such wicked projects to completion without the command of specific, tailored tools. Collaboration becomes a necessity to obtain traction in such instances, as the distinctive members of the unique project team configuration will need to heavily rely on frameworks and 'cheat-sheets' as supplements to facilitate, guide, and direct them in a constructive working path. Too often I have encountered situations where there is much good work, traction and progression underway, only to have a good chunk of the work-in-flight get squashed for reasons such as key individuals and groups not being kept in the loop for a critical decision, not informed on progress, or not solicited at a significant point to provide vital feedback. Explicit, concerted focus on the creation and usage of the <u>Stakeholder Register</u> will go a long way early and throughout the project to <u>define and give structure to the 'virtual team' of affected and interested parties.</u>

Enter the Stakeholder Register – a Short Description

The term 'Stakeholder' represents an individual, group or identifying entity (including separate organizations) that CAN Impact, or WILL BE impacted by a particular project. This includes the parties that are either involved in the project work efforts, or interested in and affected by the outcome of it.

Technically, the project can be considered successful if the project stakeholders are satisfied. However, to achieve this desired state of satisfaction, the applicable stakeholders need to be identified and analyzed with aspects of the project tailored to them with concerted care and attention throughout its lifecycle.

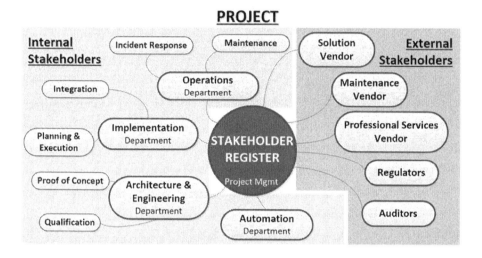

WHAT THE STAKEHOLDER REGISTER IS:

The Stakeholder Register provides a view to help clarify and determine each stakeholder's involvement, interest and expectation in the project by using people as the foundation for analysis. The highly dynamic, multi-layered nature of humans allows for varying and unbounded levels of analysis, aiding in specialized and individualized treatment of the project components' control and delivery for the stakeholders.

The Stakeholder Register allows for the effective treatment and consideration of the working and affected parties through the analysis of their attributes, such as their *roles, expectations, authorization levels, attitudes, influence, power, requirements*, and so on, as it relates to the project.

In short, the Stakeholder Register is simply a list of stakeholders in a table format, with their respective attributes defined, potentially on a single page. It is the simplest of tools but one of the most powerful and useful.

What the Stakeholder Register is NOT:

- The Stakeholder Register is commonly confused with the 'Human Resource' aspect of people management.

A fundamental clarification point is as follows:

The *Stakeholder Register* is NOT about managing the key people for the project;

Rather, it is about managing the project for the key people.*

*key people being the stakeholders

Therefore, while the Stakeholder Register CAN assist in the 'Human' aspect of Resource Management, its primary purpose is not to manage people as time-bounded resources through their cycles, skills, schedules, and so forth.

- In addition, though the Stakeholder Register has a strong affinity for the communication management side of project management, it itself is not devoted to being a communication tool.

There are other dedicated tools and techniques that exist for communication and resource management aspects of the project separate from the Stakeholder Register.

CREATION OF THE STAKEHOLDER REGISTER

There is no 'one-way' to create the Stakeholder Register. There are various considerations ranging from a number of attributes to use, to the level of detail. These are selected based on the project managers' judgement of usefulness, the organizational culture and phase of the project (a version of the Stakeholder Register contained in the project charter during the early initiation phase would be very high-level compared to a version in the planning and execution phases).

The Stakeholder Register can be built in a word document, a spreadsheet, or a software application.

How to create it:

STEP 1: IDENTIFY POTENTIAL STAKEHOLDERS – INITIAL CREATION OF REGISTER

Who is affected and interested in the project?

Sample Identification Information includes: Name, Position, and Role in the Project.

Attribute Set 1: Identification Information

Stakeholder	Role	Department	Contact Info	
Hasan	Integration SME	Implementation	Hasan@Organization.com	
Chris	Design SME	Architecture	Chris@ Organization.com	*Initial set of*
Aziz	Project Manager	Delivery	Aziz@ Organization.com	*attributes*
Hazar	Operations SME	Operations	Hazar@ Organization.com	*dedicated to*
Karim	Project Sponsor	Unit VP	Karim@ Organization.com	*'Identificatio*
Etc.				*n*
				Information'

Note – As the register is being put together for the project at hand, it is worth soliciting the potential stakeholders for their feedback on who else may be worth adding as stakeholders and why.

STEP 2: ASSESSMENT & CLASSIFICATIONS OF STAKEHOLDERS – *ELABORATE THE REGISTER*

Additionally, more detailed stakeholder attributes of interest are listed and maintained.

There can be dozens of potential attributes listed here, arguably none of which would be incorrect; however, it is important not to go overboard (stick to what is simple and useful). A separate set of **'Stakeholder Analysis'** techniques can be performed to collectively identify the value of these assessment and classification attributes, per stakeholder. Common methods of identifying the attributes values for the associated stakeholders include the use of 'Grids' and 'Maps' with accompanying weighted rankings.

Attribute Set 2: Assessment & Classification categories (examples)

Stakeholder	Expectations	Time Allocation	Internal/ External	Influence	Interest	
Hasan	Accurate Design package received from Architecture	80%	Internal	Med	High	*Set of attributes dedicated to*
Chris	Strong involvement from Operations	20%	Internal	High (decision-maker)	Med	*Assessment & Classification information, the*
Aziz	No change in Scope, Cost and Schedule	75%	Internal	Med	High	*values of which are generally*
Hazar	Solution will work in production environment upon hand-off. Training to be provided as part of Project budget.	30%	Internal	Low	Med	*determined from a separate* **Stakeholder Analysis**
Karim	Return on Investment obtained as mentioned in Project Charter	50%	Internal	High (decision-maker)	High	
Etc.	-	-	-	-	-	

EXAMPLES OF COMMON ASSESSMENT AND CLASSIFICATION ATTRIBUTES ARE AS FOLLOWS:

- Assessment information:
- Major requirements, expectations, potential for influencing outcomes, and the phase of the project life cycle where the stakeholder has the most influence or impact.
- Stakeholder classification:
- Internal/external, impact/influence/power/interest, up-ward/ downward/ outward/ sideward.

*Remember to keep it updated along the way and ensure to share it regularly in an effort to validate its accuracy.

Maintaining it is a continuous process.

USAGE OF THE STAKEHOLDER REGISTER

HOW TO USE IT:

Once created and in play, any stakeholder (as opposed to just the project manager) can leverage the stakeholder register for information and actionable usage – whether it is to treat and manage the stakeholders to their requirements, or to reach out as needed. It is a great idea for the project manager to glance at it now and then to ensure the stakeholders are being treated with appropriate consideration and to their needs. Such examples are further elaborated in the 'Use-Cases' section below.

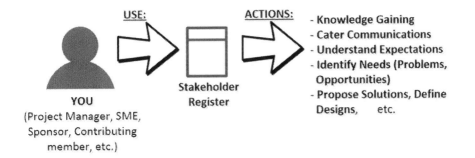

USE: Stakeholder Register ACTIONS:
- Knowledge Gaining
- Cater Communications
- Understand Expectations
- Identify Needs (Problems, Opportunities)
- Propose Solutions, Define Designs, etc.

YOU
(Project Manager, SME, Sponsor, Contributing member, etc.)

A PLETHORA OF USE-CASES AND BENEFITS:

In closing, I feel it prudent to illustrate some of the stakeholder registers' diverse array of applications. The examples below are by no means all-inclusive.

- **Transparency and Specialized Access:** anyone would have the ability to seamlessly flow through the interconnected working parts across the beast of the organization to which the project spans. The Stakeholder Register thereby allows specialized access to the significant players of the project. This also serves as a time-saver and a channel 0pener, as project team members can reference the register as a means of establishing correspondence with appropriate personnel to help them perform their tasks, especially for new-hires.

- **Aids Communication & Requirement Planning:** research shows that most failures in projects are a result of pitfalls in either communication or requirement management. The Stakeholder Register naturally helps in both of these areas; the stakeholder list as an input for the communication plan, and the 'Expectations' attribute at a high-level to reinforce top requirements.

- **A Source for Elicitation:** stakeholders can be reached as early as the initiation stage to gather thoughts, requirements and feedback.

- **Spreading of Accountability**: there is an opportunity to clarify and agree on roles on a per stakeholder basis, including the client, such as having them involved in doing more than the minimum of user acceptance testing.

- **Operational Readiness:** operations contacts should be noted to ensure specialized treatment, improving the chances of the final solution being supported and accepted post completion. Additionally, the operations contacts can provide feedback (i.e. updated checklists) to guide and ensure integration SME's are performing quality implementations.

- **Partnerships & Alliances**: monitor and track existing partnerships, and improve relationships where needed, especially with those individuals who have power or are against the project.

- **Comprehensiveness:** use the tool as a 'cross-reference' integrity check against other project management tools to ensure completeness (both ways).

- **Differentiated Treatment:** allow stakeholders to be to be treated individually and in a specialized manner as needed.

- **Governance:** identify who the decision makers are in the form of authorized approvers.

- **Lessons Learned:** help identify and avoid mistakes that happened in the past, reach out to the individuals to get their candid feedback. There is much wisdom and knowledge to be shared and people, by nature, want to help if they are approached appropriately.

- **Due Diligence and Assurance**: scorecards can subsequently be built to track assurance of due diligence per stakeholder.

- **Beyond Project Management**: as a multi-functional tool, its usefulness extends beyond project management into the worlds of operations, process and talent management.

The Stakeholder Register can be comparable to the magic in alchemy: just as alchemy facilitates the transmutation of elements from lesser essence to more precious or desirable (i.e. led to gold). **The Stakeholder Register positions the entire project's anatomy, components and compositions to be effectively matured through a systematic analysis, and differentiated treatment of the people involved and affected.**

AZIZ DURANAI

Aziz Duranai is a Senior Manager at the Royal Bank of Canada in the Network & Telecommunication Technology Infrastructure team. With over a decade of experience in the IT industry, some of his accomplishments include major network infrastructure builds and phases of related datacenter relocations, implementations of customized business-transforming software, standing up and operating various cross-functional processes, and fronting audits covering responses, creation of action plans and related execution to closure.

Aziz holds an Honours Bachelor Degree in Applied Computing from the University of Guelph, an Advanced Diploma in Wireless and Telecommunications Systems Technology, and various Certifications in technical and methodical disciplines.

As a strong supporter of systems-based methodologies, Aziz advocates wearing different hats as needed and embraces varying frameworks as enablers to achieve business and service goals within enterprise organizations. Some (overlapping) methodologies of interest include but are not limited to Quality Management Systems, Project Management, Business Analysis and Process Management.

Aziz Duranai, PMP, LSSGB, ITIL, CCNA
1173 Flagship Drive, Mississauga, Ontario, Canada, L4Y 2K3

E-mail: Aziz.Duranai@gmail.com
LinkedIn: Aziz Duranai

HITTING THE TARGET: COMMUNICATING DELIVERY READINESS TO KEY STAKEHOLDERS

TODD R. JONES

S takeholders desire – and may often require – a clear picture of the overall health of a solution leading up to the point of delivery. They want to know whether the team is on target to hit the release date and the overall quality assessment of the delivery. Comprehensive status reporting conveys meaningful data, but can often overwhelm the reader with too much text, leading to information overload. A more advantageous approach is to provide a single diagram that clearly shows the delivery fitness of the key functional areas – as defined by the stakeholders themselves.

The Delivery Readiness Chart (DRC) is that single graphic that brings into focus the most important areas of the project together with an overall indicator of progress toward the target release date. By using a standard red-yellow-green color scheme, it provides the stakeholder a simple view with a clear indication of the production readiness of each key functional area and for the release as a whole. Not only is it useful for communicating to stakeholders, but it is a valuable tool to communicate vital project status to the project team. Displaying it prominently within the team space allows for the team to constantly gauge their progress towards the delivery target.

The DRC is composed of three concentric circles. The innermost circle is shaded green, the next shaded yellow, and the outermost shaded red. Around the outside of the circles are the critical features, or functional areas, of the proposed solution– typically 10-15 items, but never more than twenty to preserve its simplistic view. These features and functional areas are defined in partnership with the business owner and the project team. Each feature and functional area is assessed on a scale of readiness – with zero being most and ten being least ready to deliver into production. The scores for each feature and functional area are then plotted on the chart with zero at the center of the circle and ten at the outer edges.

The DRC is a tool that is easy to read and understand due to its simplicity and its similarity to an actual archery target. Each plotted point symbolizes an arrow that pierces a paper target – just as my sons used to shoot at during archery club. As their technique improved, their arrows would converge towards the center of the target (i.e. the bullseye), and their completed target was a visual representation of their progress over time. In the same way, the DRC is a straightforward way to gauge the progress of a project. The points that are plotted on or near the bullseye represent features that are production-ready; outliers are easy to spot and denote functionality that is incomplete, untested, or unready for production.

A sample chart is shown in Figure x-1.

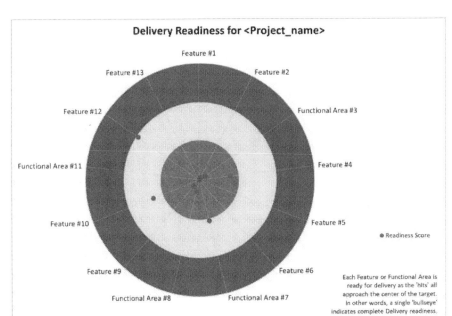

Figure x-1

Let us walk through how to build and use the chart...

The DRC can be created in various tools such as Excel, Sheets, Power-Point, or Prezi. Creating the chart in Excel is straightforward. It is a simple spider diagram with the points plotted between zero and ten with no connecting lines between each point. An image of red-yellow-green circles is added as background for the chart. The data source for the labels and point values is a two-column chart with the names of the key features/functions and their rating.

191

Sample data is shown in Figure x-2.

Functional Area		Readiness Score		Completeness (Testing or Evaluation	
Feature #1	▼	0	▼	100%	▼
Feature #2		0.2		98%	
Functional Area #3		0.6		94%	
Feature #4		2.7		73%	

Figure x-2

The simple act of creating the chart will pay dividends – as it forces stakeholders (or the product owner) to define the minimum viable product (MVP) for the release. Defining the MVP should occur regardless of what project methodology is used (i.e. traditional, agile, or some hybrid form). The features and functional areas that are being measured and reported against encompass the MVP. This provides clarity to the project team on exactly what scope is most important to deliver first, and what features can be de-prioritized to a later release, removing distractions for the team. At the very least, the DRC will help drive conversations for the features in the red. For instance, "Is feature x really needed for the current release given the remaining effort/cost?" or "Are there viable workarounds or trade-offs that can be made to hold to the current schedule?"

One of the most critical factors to consider when implementing the DRC is defining what to use as the measurement of progress – i.e. what objective metric is used to determine where the points are plotted on the graph. The more objective the metric, the more accurate and repeatable the chart will be throughout the project's life-cycle. It is also easier to calculate and update the chart during each reporting period.

Examples of quantitative measurements include:

- % of story points delivered (# delivered / # total)
- % of use cases completed (# completed / # total)
- % of test cases passed (# passed / # total)
- % of defects remaining (# open defects / # total defects)

It should be noted that percentages work very well as they easily translate into plottable points, but may need to be inverted so the points advance towards the center of the graph. An example of a qualitative measure would be a survey of the product owner or project team of their perception of the readiness of each feature.

As with other information radiators, the DRC should remain visible to the project team from the time of its first communication up to final delivery. Visualizing progress on a regular frequency is extremely important when following a traditional or waterfall methodology – due to the length of elapsed time between milestones and delivery points – to keep the team's forward momentum and active engagement. Stakeholders should expect to see the DRC at regular intervals just like they would during weekly or monthly status reporting on a traditional project.

For an agile team, the chart should be posted daily, either physically within the team's space or on a virtual wall, to keep the team well-informed of progress during a shortened delivery cycle. Even though stakeholders are likely more in tune to the team's progress, the DRC should still be distributed at least weekly during the delivery cycle.

Agile teams should create the DRC during sprint planning, documenting the scope items selected to be delivered during that sprint. The updated DRC is shown during the feature demo of a sprint, where that feature would reside in the bullseye of the chart indicating that scope is completed. Plotted points outside of the bullseye would clearly evidence scope items that were not yet completed.

The DRC can be used with a Kanban board. As cards move from column to column the points would move from the outer circles to the inner circles converging on the bullseye – signifying complete.

The DRC can also be used in a program setting. Within a program, each point would still signify key features regardless of the project team responsible for its delivery. Alternatively, each point could represent a project team, where their collective contributions are consolidated towards a final solution. This is especially useful when each team is expected to deliver their portion of scope at about the same sprint. The whole solution will eventually converge on the bullseye indicating overall delivery preparedness for the entire program.

The DRC gives the project sponsor, project steering committee, and other stakeholders an instant view of the overall health of the project. It can also indicate the risk of not meeting an upcoming milestone or sprint delivery. The DRC should be used to prompt healthy conversation between the project or program manager and the business stakeholder(s) about the overall readiness of the delivery. For example, the DRC can be used as a catalyst for MVP discussions:

- Do the features that are ready for delivery provide adequate functionality to users?
- Will it provide enough business value to warrant release?
- What is the risk of releasing to market without all the planned scope not yet ready?

This leads to multiple 'what-if' scenarios where the stakeholders should be able to qualify, and if possible quantify the risk of not delivering full functionality, and determine the benefit of delivering partial functionality that may include necessary manual work to defects or incomplete functionality. Essentially, do the benefits of waiting for a higher quality solution outweigh the cost of waiting to bring the product to its ultimate quality level?

Communication of status to stakeholders is not negotiable, and there are many ways for project managers to do it. The delivery readiness chart is an excellent method to effectively convey current progress and provide a comprehensive view of the overall delivery fitness of the solution in a single diagram. Using charting tools like Excel or Sheets, it is easy to create from data that is readily available for the critical features or functional areas that were defined and prioritized at the beginning of the project. The simple graphic eliminates the need for stakeholders to wade through paragraphs of text to comprehend status and know whether the project/program will hit the target.

TODD R. JONES

 Todd has a diverse background - as a developer, architect, project manager, and testing leader – directing dozens of business and technology projects with a proven track record of satisfied sponsors and team members. He has extensive experience applying traditional project management methodologies as well as iterative and agile approaches at Westfield Insurance.

Todd is an accomplished speaker on various topics related to project management and testing. He is a recent past speaker at PMI Global Congress, PMI Leadership Institute, STPCon, DevOps East, PMI NJ Symposium, and multiple other PMI Chapter events across the United States.

Todd is an active member of the PMI Northeast Ohio chapter (PMINEO), where he has volunteered since 2010. He currently serves on the chapter's Governance Board, providing strategic leadership to deliver increased member value. Todd is also a recent graduate of PMI's Leadership Institute Master Class and was the recipient of the Dr. Harold Kerzner Project Management Excellence Award in 2016.

Todd is certified as a Project Management Professional (PMP®) and an Agile Certified Practitioner (PMI-ACP®). He also holds Certified Scrum Master (CSM®) designation from the Scrum Alliance. Todd graduated from Grove City College with a B.S. Computer Science and Mathematics.

Connect with Todd at www.linkedin.com/in/toddrjones

PROJECT LEADERSHIP: VALUING PEOPLE TO OWN, SHARE AND PROTECT GREAT WORK

AMBER MCMILLAN

World-renowned leadership guru, Warren Bennis, and his co-author, Burt Nanus, concluded that "managers are people who **do things right** and leaders are people who **do the right things**." (Emphasis added.)

I have perseverated on that statement over the course of my project management career and while applying the core concepts of our professional body of knowledge, I have found it to be true. To **do things right** means to follow the rules. To **do the right things** means recognizing that there is more than one right way to accomplish work. In my experience, when project work is done under the assumption that there is only one right way to approach the work, it scarcely transcends to all it can be. As project managers, we are called upon to use expert judgement in how we manage work. But, does that mean doing things right?

As an only child growing up in the shadow of successful, entrepreneurial parents, I spent much of my time focused on doing things right. To add value to how people viewed me and to build self-confidence, this became an essential part of my professional experience. However, my fixation on rightness became my greatest hurdle, and after many years of fighting to gain more power and influence through working 'righter', I quit. I gave up the fight to prove myself as a project manager who did the right work and turned my attention towards becoming a project leader. I had observed, over time, that position and authority had little to do with leadership and I watched effective project managers lead through tough situations with or without authority, finding a way to inspire people to great work. Furthermore, the work was not always accomplished by doing things right but by doing the right things.

MEASURING PROJECT SUCCESS

We are told in project management that good communication is the greatest measure of success. I would argue that how you treat people on projects could be an even greater measure because when people are managed like parts of a machine and controlled to assigned tasks, their work suffers. When a project manager masquerades as a leader by exercising leadership and strategy tactics only to manipulate people for their own selfish gain, the work suffers. When people lack confidence in authority or feel undervalued, their work ceases to be effective.

In my own career, I have felt the sting of both being undervalued and manipulated. I recall one particular instance when a manager called me into their office, gently closed the door and whispered of a great underhandedness afoot in the organization waged against me. They promised to protect me if I would take on a new role, working on a special project only they controlled. Days later, I discovered this manager had crafted the story out of thin air, using my trust in them to manipulate me into doing their work. It created a toxic environment that caused me to lose confidence in that authority and I let the quality of my work suffer. Although I remained on that project for eight more months, I completed tasks with neither the enthusiasm nor the inspiration to accomplish great work. The work became a job and a paycheck and the reality I faced in that situation helped me pivot my career. The emotional and physical toll it took forced me to look at project management and leadership differently. As a manager, I was successful at controlling situations to reach objectives, refining systems and processes, and assigning tasks to people in the right direction. However, being on the receiving end of those same approaches made me look towards the true nature of leadership, and I had to accept that failure could be a step to success; motivation comes from being trusted and people are always deserving of respect and honesty.

EFFECTIVE LEADERSHIP

The most effective leadership uses different approaches in different situations. Situational leadership is a style developed and studied by Kenneth Blanchard and Paul Hersey that refers to leaders or managers adjusting their style to fit the development level of those they are trying to influence. They ask themselves and the people they are leading, 'Why are we doing this?' 'How can we do this better?' and 'What can we learn from this?' all while communicating their values and goals. They give people space to use their own talent to achieve success and they admit freely what they know along with what they do not. They demonstrate a broad range of soft skills like social and emotional intelligence, and they present these skills based on the situations they find themselves in. In action, situational leadership uses both influence and transparency to build trust. This creates value for both the leader and those they lead.

BUILDING VALUE

As every human has the autonomous right to place value where they believe it exists, effective project leaders know they cannot force or coerce people to value what they want them to. In my own project leadership, I'm committed to the following three steps to valuing people to see success:

#1 OWN IT

In order to create that value, I first **own** the work myself. Beyond writing a charter or overseeing the project plan, it is personal ownership that means taking responsibility and assuming liability. As a project manager, I must not only consider the benefits associated with project, but also the costs, and still be willing to admit my insecurities. The good, the bad and the ugly - of what the project work might bring - can be tough to digest, but not talking openly about the realities of the work is immature. A great leader owns the whole story with the bad and ugly parts seen as opportunities to collaborate in mitigating the fallout, calculating risk and devising strategies to stand strong in the midst of questions, scrutiny and objection.

#2 SHARE IT

After owning both the positives and negatives of the project, I **share** what I know. Early on in my career, struggling to do the 'right' work, I kept much of the detailed project information to myself. I was great at assigning tasks and leading people to follow directions but I was often left to do the work myself when they did not feel trusted to do the work the way they knew how. Having personally experienced how it feels to be manipulated at work, I understood the need to lead with transparency no matter how vulnerable it made me feel. Seemingly counterintuitive, without a doubt, being transparent is the most authentic way to relate to the people side of the work. It inspires collaboration and when a leader tells the truth, they are more likely to get the truth - which means risk registers can be built to reflect reality and project decisions can be made based on fact and not fiction.

Leadership transparency derails suspicion. When a leader can discuss worst-case scenarios candidly, it is disarming to the people who are affected. It levels the playing field and invites people to become co-authors in the solutions. A leader that communicates mistruths or half-truths is simply immature. Effective leaders own and share the whole story. When they do, it fosters trust in teammates, staff, sponsors and stakeholders. It also invites people to own the work themselves so they begin to place their own value in the project.

#3 PROTECT IT

Finally, when the project work is strategized collaboratively to reflect the good, the bad and the ugly of what is ahead, I make my remaining role to **protect** the work involved in the project. As a testament to collaboration and trust, I know the work itself is never more important than the people who represent it. And, with everyone involved placing value where they believe it exists, I need to lead in a way deserving of that value. I work to earn it by owning the truth, sharing the truth, and inviting collaboration. When teammates, staff, sponsors and stakeholders feel valued, they share that value in the form of high quality work, agility and flexibility.

FINAL THOUGHTS

While I have found these three steps highly effective, there are exceptions to its success. Some teammates and stakeholders have used the vulnerability I practice to leverage collaboration and transparency for their own selfish gain. My experience has taught me that the more I accept these moments as opportunities to understand more of human nature, the less they seem to happen. As the wise poet, Maya Angelou, once said, "Do the best you can until you know better; then, when you know better, do better." I use each turn of events and every step of the way to learn and grow in my understanding of the better not the 'right' way to lead.

AMBER MCMILLAN

Amber is a diversely skilled professional with a unique approach for innovating and leading projects in various environments. With experience in all aspects of project, change and people management as well as operations and organizational strategy, she is committed to the highest of standards, works diligently to create positive working environments and is motivated by her own contagious enthusiasm.

With tangible credentials and over 25 years of experience in both profit and not-for-profit environments, she is well equipped to contribute her skill set in complex organizations in need of dynamic and proprietary services.

Amber is Executive Director of Rogers Society, a not-for-profit community centre in Victoria, BC specializing in child and youth care services as well as community programming. She is also an Executive Educator throughout Western Canada instructing on Leadership, Communication and Stakeholder Management, a conference speaker and workshop teacher in all aspects of project, change and people management and Past President at PMI Vancouver Island Chapter. She holds a PMP (Project Management Professional designation), Change Management Certified in Prosci ADKAR and a CVA (Certified Volunteer Administrator).

Amber McMillan, PMP, Prosci ADKAR CMC , CVA
amber@ambermcmillan.com
ambermcmillan.com
LinkedIn: ambermcmillancom
Twitter: @ambermcm

STRATEGIC ALIGNMENT

WAEL RAMADAN

As organizations adapt and restructure in order to survive and grow, it is vital for project managers to understand the implications of the notion of strategic alignment. It is one thing to say that a project is done right, but is it another thing to say that the right project is done right? Achieving the basic project objectives of scope, time, cost, and quality, meets only the simplest and lowest level of project success. A second and higher level of success is defined when the right project is done right. The right project is an endeavor that is aligned with the strategic path of the organization and hence brings it closer to achieving its strategic objectives. Strategic alignment not only enables project managers to define different levels of project success, but also provides them with better insights into trade-off decision making among project priorities. Most organizations are constrained with limited resources; therefore, selecting the right projects for implementation is important for driving organizational success. There is a positive correlation between strategic alignment and organizational competitive advantage, and strategic alignment enables project managers to define the track before asking their team members to stay on it.

In order for us to better understand the notion of strategic alignment let us consider Diagram 1 below:

Diagram 1: Illustrating the Link between Project Management and Strategy.

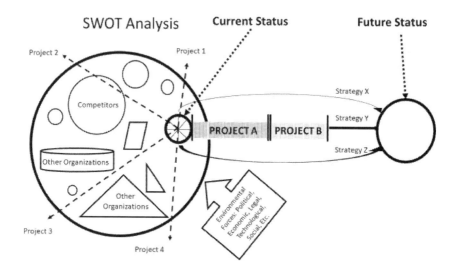

Diagram 1 illustrates the strategic planning process and the link between project management and strategic planning. Strategic planning simply answers three questions for us:

1. Where are we now (current status)?
2. Where do we want to be in the future (future status)?
3. How do we go from here to there (strategy)?

Project management is an output of strategic planning, and projects are the vehicles of implementing strategic plans. Therefore, strategic plans are decomposed into projects that take the organization from where it is, to where it wants to be in the future. We can define strategy as the way in which the organization utilizes its organizational resources that are usually rare and unique, to achieve its strategic objectives. Strategy sustains the business, whereas projects deliver their objectives and then terminate. Strategy could be proactive or reactive and could also be described as an art of organizational survival. The success of strategy is dependent on how well it is implemented. Strategy implementation makes 75% of its success while strategy development makes only 25%.

Setting strategic organizational objectives is a successor to the process of environmental scan. This environmental scan is both external and internal and it is known as SWOT analysis. It includes scanning external factors that affect the organization such as: economic, legal, social, technological, environmental, and political factors. In the external scan, opportunities and threats are identified. Opportunities examples include: growth in the market share and, joint ventures and acquisition of other firms; and threats examples include: competition, changes in regulations, new and better products. In the internal scan, factors of strength and weakness are identified. Examples of strength factors include: a large talent pool, many certified project managers, having many PMOs, reputation, financial stability, brand name, strategic locations, and so on. The lack of any of the strength factors becomes a weakness. It is the project managers' responsibility to inform themselves of the strategic goals and objectives and the trends that affect organizational performance, in order to understand the organizational priorities and to be able to implement the trade-off decision making among project objectives.

Whenever a project manager develops a business case, a proposal, or a charter, it must be shown that the proposed project will bring the organization closer to achieving its strategic goals. The strategic goals could be short-tem, mid-term, or long-term goals.

If the proposed project is not aligned with the organizational strategic goals, then it will not bring the organization closer to achieving its strategic goals. In Diagram 1: Project 1, Project 2, Project 3, and Project 4 are not strategically aligned, and they take the organization in a different direction away from its strategic goals if these projects are selected and implemented. So, if we implement these projects right, on time, and on budget, they will meet our first definition of success, which states that success is to do a project right. However, Project A and Project B are strategically aligned and they will bring the organization closer to achieving its strategic goals; if implemented, Projects A and B will meet our second definition of success, which states that success is to do the right project right. Organizations that have maturity in the implementation of project management methodology and best practices would be able to do the right project right, over and over again, and this is the highest level of success. Usually, organizations that have one or more (PMO) managers are able to meet this third and highest level of success. Strategic alignment is also a necessity for organizations that are not project-based.

A critical success factor in strategic alignment and to achieving project success is the role of an important stakeholder. This stakeholder is described as follows: harvester of promised benefits, owner of the business case, governor of the project, champion of the project, and "a friend in high places" to the project manager. What do you think? Which stakeholder are we talking about here? It is of course the sponsor.

When it comes to project selection, there are essential questions that must be asked to ensure that we are selecting and defining the right project, and these questions are:

- Why are we doing the project? (This question is answered by the Business Case.)

- Are we doing this project the right way? (This question is answered by the Project Strategy.)
- What do we have to do in this project? (This question is answered by the Project Scope.)
- Are we sure this is the right project to be selected? (This question is answered by the Strategic Alignment.)

One final question that comes to mind is what would happen to projects that are not strategically aligned if they are selected? Well, one consequence would be that these projects would be targets for elimination when funding is tight.

WAEL RAMADAN

Dr. Wael Ramadan is a Professor of Project Management and Strategy at Pilon School of Business in Canada. He is the recipient of seven academic scholarships including the prestigious Fulbright Scholarship. Wael is an internationally experienced consultant, educator, author and speaker.

Wael lead the Board of Directors of Project Management Institute (PMI) Lakeshore Chapter as President (2013-2014). He is currently an Editorial Board Member of Universal Journal of Management (UJOM), and Chair of Advisory Committee for MLM Graduate Program at Ryerson University, and he is the author of the book: "The Asset That Money Can't Buy".

As an entrepreneur, Wael co-founded and led two manufacturing businesses from scratch to market leadership, and he enjoyed negotiating and winning two national bids. As a management and training consultant, Wael provides his expertise for various public and private sector clients across the globe. Wael has designed and delivered 1000's of hours of PMP Exam Prep training and he is a frequent speaker at PMI events and at other professional organizations.

Wael is a certified Lean Six Sigma Black Belt (LSSBB), LRQA - ISO Quality Auditor (2000), and Project Management Professional (PMP) since 2001. His academic background includes B.Eng. in Biochemical Engineering form University College London (UK), MBA from Maastricht

School of Management (Netherlands), and PhD form Cleveland State University (US).

Wael Ramadan, B.Eng., MBA, PhD, PMP, LSSBB.
Professor of Project Management and Strategy,
Pilon School of Business,
4180 Duke of York Blvd.,
Mississauga, ON L5B0G5.
Mobile: 905 334 9018
Email: waelaljerashy@gmail.com
LinkedIn: https://www.linkedin.com/in/dr-wael-ramadan-pmp-lssbb-2940a123/

HOW DO PROJECT MANAGERS MAKE BEST FAST DECISIONS?

SAEED ROKOOEI

Decision-making is one of the key responsibilities of project managers and plays a critical role in the success of projects. In the classical decision-making approach, the issue is determined, and all possible responses are identified. In the next step and based on pre-determined objectives, a set of criteria will be specified to evaluate the options or responses. Filtering the options results in the best option being chosen for implementation and possibly, new decisions are identified. One main resource that this process requires is time. Project managers, independently and collectively, make their decisions within a meaningful timeframe. However, an abundance of time is not always available. In fact, many situations inevitably necessitate immediate decisions. In these cases, the processing stage has limited access to the supplementary resources, tools, and methods and therefore, classical decision-making will not be a viable approach. Hence, a new model should be designed for decision-making under time pressure. This chapter briefly presents the decision-making tools and approaches (applied by project managers) to address the severity of time pressure and reach optimal outcomes. In addition, the following items demonstrate how the personal characteristics of project managers play a role in instant decision-making processes.

DIFFERENT APPROACHES DURING TIME-PRESSURED DECISION-MAKING

1.USING PRIOR KNOWLEDGE

Utilizing prior knowledge is a short and reliable path for project managers. The first reaction of project managers through instant decision-making is to consider if they have experienced similar situations so they can anticipate a process and act accordingly. This prior knowledge most often comes from practical sources and not theoretical ones. Under time pressure, the tendency to find a quick response hinders project managers to think about the information and summarize theoretical conclusions; in this situation, practical knowledge is a convenient method to create situational parallelism. In addition to their ease of use, prior knowledge references are less risky, as they are typically authenticated by external sources. However, the unique natures of projects, especially the aspects that are subject to judgement, make it harder to make historical-based decisions. In order to use this approach in instant decision-making, project managers should review the processes of similar projects beforehand.

2. ANALYZING AVAILABLE DATA

In encountering instant decision-making situations, project managers use the available data as an input into their decision-making. This approach entails two main points. First, the availability of data is the subject of discussion, as it directly relates to time - the more time, the more data available. Therefore, given limited time, project managers typically have access to limited – and mainly high-level – data. The data can be unwritten or close at hand. A summary of project performance or a management dashboard becomes a crucial and reliable tool. The second point is the importance of project managers' thinking abilities. Project managers should have strong analytical skills to effectively make decisions.

3. CONSULTING WITH OTHER TEAM MEMBERS

Having an accessible and knowledgeable team is a great advantage for any project manager. The existence and structure of such teams heavily depend on the size and nature of projects. Specialized organizations often have a (PMO), which acts as the heart of project management functions. Larger projects allow the project team to include more people. Smaller organizations or non-professional clients may not have a formal project management office or division, but more likely, there is a pseudo-project management team that handles project planning, execution, and control. To have the team members' input, project managers must have very easy and swift communication channels.

4. RELYING ON INTUITION

The tendency to make decisions intuitively is routine for many project managers. Although there is no conspicuous, calculated reasoning, behind project managers' instincts, intuition-based decision-making works well in many situations. An example of this phenomenon is first-glance shopping, in which either sufficient pricing data is not available or enough time is not given to understand current pricing. Intuition is a divergent point for some project manager professionals, such that categorizing intuition under a particular decision-making methodology. However, this unconscious process is not a haphazard action. Pieces of information, little by little, provide solid insights towards project aspects that can be used as a foundation for further decisions under time pressure.

5. ESTIMATING POSSIBLE CONSEQUENCES

Knowing the possible outcomes of decisions helps project managers to take different approaches. Sometimes project managers are unable to distinguish between different options that they have in order to make correct decisions. Available information appears to be not at a level that a project manager needs to effectively act or react; however, it is easier – less risky – to choose some options that might result in less waste, less cost, or fewer problems. Under time pressure, project managers tend to bring an estimate of possible consequences into play and roughly perform a shallow and quick risk analysis. Moreover, among various options with similar calculated outcomes (the multiplication of probability and value), project managers tend to take options with lower values.

6. ASKING UPPER MANAGEMENT WHAT TO DO

Getting feedback or comments from upper management is a method to deal with time pressure that works well for many project managers, especially those less experienced. Although it might look embarrassing for project managers to refer to their supervision at critical moments and request guidance, this approach should not be disvalued. Learning project management skills is an iterative process, and project managers should embrace every opportunity that they get to acquire knowledge and recognition from more experienced people. Entrusting senior managers on instant decisions is a prudent approach that project managers can take; although, the availability of upper management in a short period of time is always an issue to consider.

7. CONSULTING WITH EXTERNAL EXPERTS

The availability of input resources for decisions made under time pressure is always a major challenge for project managers, and, thus, exploring ways to increase such resources is a useful project management activity. Referring to external experts is a valuable approach that can help project managers to pass through instances of quick decisions, especially with the fact that these situations are often accompanied by a shortage of internal human resources. However, it should be noted that external experts are more suitable to provide feedback and comments on those aspects of decisions that do not need detailed project information. Content knowledge gaps or stuck-in-box situations are better times to consider external viewpoints.

8. REFERRING TO ONLINE SOURCES

The advent of information technology has enhanced project management tools and methods, and online sources have become a major source of information for project managers. Many online websites and applications supply a great deal of information to users, and it seems this widespread trend will continue. Online sources provide project managers with plenty of categorized and specific inputs in the blink of an eye and, therefore, are very handy under time pressure. Nonetheless, project managers should always consider two main criteria in selecting online sources: authentication and brevity. The abundance of unauthenticated data causes distractions, especially under time pressure. Project managers must know which sources are reliable and how they need to extract data efficiently.

9. ASSIGNING THE TASK TO OTHERS

Involving other people in project issues may decrease the intensity of the decision-making process. This method is useful when a project manager feels anxiety over available time and is unable to perform well. In addition to normal activities that a project manager should do during the decision-making process, a state of instability comes along as a result of time pressure, which exacerbates circumstances. Coping with all logical and emotional aspects of fast decisions is not an easy task, and having another person, such as a team member, a colleague, or a professional, may alleviate the situation. Additionally, it brings a new perspective to the decision-making process.

10. PHASING THE DECISION

Phasing decisions is helpful when relatively large or important decisions are being made. The pressure of time makes the line between different elements of the decision subject blurry, and it misleads project managers to see the decision subject as a bundle and entices them to respond as soon as possible. However, scrutinizing the subject may reveal that only one or a few aspects need an immediate response. Phasing decisions allows project managers to obtain more time and make decisions with less anxiety.

11. BUYING TIME BY PUTTING OFF THE DECISION

Postponing decision-making can be considered as the most passive response to the situation, but it is not always the worst action. Under time pressure, as with other impacts, project managers may feel the necessity of a quick response; but, how quick? The estimated proper response time is a product of many factors. Of these, the project managers' perception is a major factor. Therefore, the estimated duration may be greater than the real one. This may force the project managers to make a decision quicker than is actually needed.

SAEED ROKOOEI

Saeed Rokooei is an assistant professor of Building Construction Science at Mississippi State University. His professional experience includes responsibilities as an architect, project scheduler, and project manager in both private firms and public organizations since 2003. Other responsibilities include management consultant and president of a construction engineering and management firm. He has also conducted several research projects and taught project management courses since 2006.

Saeed obtained his bachelor's degree in Architectural Engineering and then continued his studies in Construction and Project Management. He completed his Master of Science in Management Information Systems at the University of Nebraska at Omaha and Ph.D. in Engineering at the University of Nebraska-Lincoln. His research project, entitled "Project Management Education Research Excellence within Cyber-Infrastructure Environment", investigated the use of simulation for project management education and consisted of two simulation applications. Saeed's research areas include project management education, creativity and sustainability, simulation, visualization, and data analytics.

Saeed is a PMP holder and a PMI member since 2012. Before moving to Mississippi, he served as the Director of Advanced Education at the PMI Heartland Chapter. Saeed is currently the Vice President-Membership and Recruiting at the PMI-CMS Chapter.

FINE-TUNING YOUR SCHEDULES

KATHI SONIAT

I have had the unusual circumstance of having three different jobs in 2019 all before the month of June. My contract ended early in the year and my next job turned out poorly. Shortly afterward, I was fortunate enough to land my dream job. Job #1 was a large International company where my "team" of seven was one of two IT teams who managed the logistics software company-wide. Job #2 was a regional company with an IT department of eleven at the corporate headquarters where I was located. Job #3 is an entrepreneurial software development company where the total organization numbers eleven.

Each time, at each job, I was hired to create/expand the process, improve schedule accuracy, manage and grow resources, and deliver a quality product.

Even though each company was incredibly different in size and breadth, the projects, processes, tracking and resource needs were particularly similar. The area's in which I was able to make the principal initial impact was in time tracking and priority setting.

TIME

Time is one aspect that cannot truly be negotiated. As project managers or operations managers, we must make efficient use of time. We must estimate and track our time in detail and know that time will pass regardless of how wisely we make use of it.

Besides the standard projects and tasks, are you capturing the following?

- Holidays
- Standing meetings
- Time away from the office for travel, training and so on
- Support, if appropriate
- Time spent for continuous improvement (may be separate from projects)

At company #1 they were only tracking "development/task time" when I arrived. When our top developer only showed 30 hours on the calendar, the business side wanted an urgent task completed that used up the remaining 10 hours. What they did not realize is he had one day's vacation scheduled and a two2-hour training planned. I changed the tracking to include *all time* to better represent true availability and set appropriate expectations.

At company #3 they were not tracking holidays and recurring meetings in their project scheduler. Their recurring meetings included a weekly meeting with each customer – so this was not an inconsequential number. They were also having a hard time meeting their deadlines. When I added all these "known" times commitments – the equivalent of one-and-a-half-person time was consumed until the end of the year. This was a real eye-opener. With this large amount of time not accounted for, it was very difficult to meet their existing schedules.

This company has a 30-minute daily meeting which included all employees. For each person that is 2.5 hours per week – for eleven people that is 27.5 hours per week. With 25 weeks left in the year this on specific meeting accounts for 687.5 hours. That is equal to 17 weeks for one person; a huge time consumption that was not previously accounted for!

GETTING EVEN MORE GRANULAR: TEAM SKILL LEVEL AND PLAN FOR GROWTH

The traditional work breakdown structure will list each task, time estimate, and resource assigned. Do you assign the same estimate for each task regardless of resource? A less experienced resource will most likely take longer than a more skilled resource. Do you assign "stretch" tasks to your junior team members and allow extra time for learning and research?

Do you allow time for continuous improvement? Regardless of the company / team size you should allow time for improvement activities that will make your team more efficient and effective. Company #3 is a software development company so making updates and improvements to our product is key in staying competitive. We must balance the customer requests which have a direct payback with those items that we know need improving and will provide long-term gains and improve customer satisfaction.

TIME MANAGEMENT:

We have looked specifically at time and detailed tracking for accuracy; but, time management is a key aspect of project management and involves skills such as planning, setting goals, and prioritizing for better performance.

An effective high-level method of providing a visual of your annual plan is a project roadmap. This will present an overview of the most important components and milestones in a one-page format. Setting out your timeline with focus on your different workstreams and estimated milestones can be the baseline for more detailed planning later in the year.

At company #1 there was an exceptional formal roadmap system in place- but sometimes it was not completed until March – well into the year. I began working for company #3 in June. I put the existing projects into a roadmap so we could see our project load for the remainder of the year. An "update" to a new software release for a customer was one of the projects listed. Additional customers were named as also needing updates when I had the team review the roadmap. By the time we were finished we had added all thirteen customers who had this software as requiring an update. This brought us well into the following year and again was a real eye-opener. It was also a good start on next year and sparked an idea to make updating customers more efficient. When we must schedule new work, we pull up the roadmap and decide where it would best fit and its impact on existing projects.

There are tools that specialize in creating roadmaps, but I find that Visio does a fantastic job.

PRIORITIES: TIME WELL SPENT

THE URGENT VS. IMPORTANT MATRIX

	URGENT	NOT URGENT
IMPORTANT	**I** crisis pressing problems projects with close deadline	**II** preparation planning new opportunities relationship building
NOT IMPORTANT	**III** interruptions some calls some emails some meetings	**IV** busy work some calls some emails time wasters

The above chart is most likely familiar to the experienced project manager. What may not be as well-known is how to manage each quadrant.

Quadrant I: Urgent & Important – Needs to be managed, but you want to minimize activities that fall here. Is there a problem in your process or product or is it a training issue or a perspective problem? This may be where managing expectations can prevent an important item from turning urgent.

Quadrant II: Not Urgent & Important – This is where you want to work. This is your sweet spot. The work is important and where you gain your most value. As these items are not urgent there is lower stress and your resources can work to their full potential.

Quadrant III: Urgent & Not Important – You want to avoid this quadrant at all costs. Not important yet urgent means these activities should not have your attention. Notice that emails fall here. An aspect of that is "interruption" from your current task. Turn off notifications and create a schedule for checking your email. Set a specific time that you will respond to emails and let people know when that is, so they know when to expect a response. For example, I respond to emails from two – four p.m. each afternoon. Have a system to identify urgent emails that may not be able to wait. Meetings are also listed here. Is your expertise required in the meetings you are invited to? Could you delegate this to a team member? One of the hardest aspects of this quadrant is someone else may be expressing urgency. This viewpoint could be contagious and, you must reasonably and calmly explain why this is also not important.

Quadrant IV: Not Urgent & Not Important – Activities in this quadrant should be limited. The whole point is to not waste time and to complete work which provides value, and is important.

If you analyze those items which may be "habits" (at your company or within in your team) you may discover that you are doing some things because "they have always been done that way" – not because they add value. You may find that instead of two or three resources attending a meeting with a customer, one could suffice. An additional time-saving move is to schedule 30-minute meetings rather than 60 minutes by default. Set an agenda, stick to it, and make good use of your time.

Empower your team to make superior use of their time. An efficient team is priceless.

KATHI SONIAT

Kathi Soniat is a Senior Project Manager at Solutions ITW, an entrepreneurial IT software company in downtown Greenville, SC. With a background in programming and favoring manufacturing companies she has worked at such as companies as AFCO, Nutra, Park Seed, BMW and Michelin in Upstate SC.

Kathi holds bachelor's degrees in Music Education and Computer Science from University of South Carolina.

Kathi is active in the PMI Palmetto Chapter. She has volunteered on the Symposium Team, as VP of Membership, President and currently serves as Past President. She serves on the board of directors of Hearts in Harmony an equine-assisted learning organization which uses horses to help troubled teens, foster children, veterans with PTSD and women in recovery.

E-mail: ksoniat77@gmail.com
LinkedIn: www.linkedin.com/pub/kathi-soniat-pmp/8/732/149/

THE IMPORTANCE OF SELF-AWARENESS FOR PROJECT MANAGERS

SOHAIL THAKER

INTRODUCTION

As project managers, we help organizations and individuals navigate change. So, we must understand the emotions people experience when facing change. We must know how to provide support. Before helping others with their change journeys, we ought to know our own strengths and weaknesses and how they impact each of us as a leader. Are you self-aware and have you developed your emotional intelligence?

The most challenging aspect of project management is not time management, budget, or scope—it is managing people: others and ourselves. Many of us know our strengths, but few of us look at our weaknesses. Without a balanced view of one's self, it is difficult to be authentic and to build trusted relationships, which is the key to leading effective change.

Want a high-performing team? Become a self-aware project manager who focuses on relationships as well as tasks, foster a collaborative team culture, and help all members bring their own strengths to the table; navigate the team through conflicts, and nurture the project team.

EMOTIONALLY UNAWARE

Sheldon from "Big Bang Theory" is a great example of how an emotionally unaware person acts. He is clearly intelligent (he has a high IQ), but Sheldon lacks many social skills required for creating healthy working teams. Furthermore, he is easily triggered emotionally when he is uncomfortable.

What sets you off? Think about those times when you let your emotions control you and you acted inappropriately. Maybe you did something and were embarrassed when you realized others were watching. Maybe you were challenged with a task that made you uncomfortable and you lost your temper. Any of these scenarios can cause a person to lose control.

As a project manager, you need to think about the importance of remaining calm, even when you do not feel calm. People will be watching your actions and behaviors, and as a leader, you are a role model for your teams. If, when uncomfortable, you "lose your cool" you set a norm for the team.

The primary reason employees leave companies is poor management—people do not quit organizations, they quit managers. We need to develop our self-awareness so we can lead by example.

HOW SELF-AWARENESS HELPED ME BE A BETTER PROJECT MANAGER

I want to share a personal story that illustrates my journey towards self-awareness. Early in my career, I excelled at avoiding conflict. I was an expert at it, and I avoided it at all costs. During projects, I avoided dealing with angry people and bullies. Sometimes, this caused negative things to happen. My fear of confrontations and anger negatively affected me and my teams.

I was fortunate, then, to take courses that taught me to look at my emotions. Through workshops, I learned to deal with my anger. More importantly, I learned why I avoided anger.

As a child, I watched my parents go through a bitter divorce. They fought a lot, enduring the pain of an ending marriage. As a child, I concluded that anger is a terrible emotion. In fact, I tried to avoid strong emotions all together. As an adult, I began the healing that enabled me to take ownership of this part of myself. I became more comfortable around anger.

At the time, I was working with a manager who did not want to participate in my project. I warned him, gently, several times, that I would escalate the issue if he did not cooperate. Soon, we were in a meeting with his boss, and I brought up the issue. He lost his temper with me and shouted at me. Previously, I would have backed off and tried to avoid the confrontation, but with my new awareness, I stood my ground. I recognized I had already tried being nice with him and faced him head on. I challenged his assertions, allowing my own anger to rise in a controlled way. By the end of the argument, he stormed out of the room.

Days later, I reached out to him, and he told me he had never expected a consultant to get as passionate about their work as I had. He respected me for challenging him and not backing down, and he committed to work on the project. We are friends to this day.

I am less afraid of anger and strong emotions because I faced my own emotional story. This made me a more effective project manager. I learned that, in evaluating myself, I need to recognize my weaknesses just as much as my strengths.

WHAT IS SELF-AWARENESS?

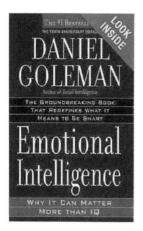

Self-awareness is conscious knowledge of one's own character, feelings, motives, and desires. Daniel Goleman, who wrote the book *Emotional Intelligence*, describes self-awareness as the cornerstone to emotional intelligence. It is the ability to monitor one's emotions and thoughts moment to moment and is the key to understanding oneself better, being at peace with oneself, and proactively managing one's thoughts, emotions, and behaviors. It is about understanding your personality including:

- Your strengths and weaknesses
- Your thoughts and beliefs
- Your motivations and emotions

It is about understanding how you react in different situations. When you see yourself clearly and understand what drives you, you can modify your approach to each situation. I learned how I reacted to anger and then I learned how to better manage my approach to confrontations. When you see yourself clearly, you can be more confident and creative, make better decisions, and build better relationships.

If you can understand how others see you, you can be more empathetic and take other perspectives into account. This makes you a better project manager.

The education system in the early 2000s picked up ideas from the book *Emotional Intelligence* to teach children to express and manage their emotions. I had a conversation with my daughter, Maya, when she was eleven years old. I asked her to tell me what she knew about emotions. She responded,

> *Daddy, I know that we have to work things out. We have to take the time to listen to each other and try to understand, even if we do not agree. We need to know when we are angry, but I know we cannot take it out on the other person.*

Maya was very aware of her emotions and able to describe and label them, manage them, and work through issues with others in emotionally charged situations. This is the value of building self- awareness.

SELF-AWARENESS EXERCISE

I want you to take a minute to complete an exercise to help you develop some insights. Grab some paper and answer the following questions. Do not over-think it—just put down your first responses to each question:

1. Think of a person, real or fictional, who you admire. Write down the person's name on your sheet. What are positive aspects of that character? Write down three to five of their positive characteristics (strength, morals, attitude, for example).
2. Think of a person, real or fictional, who irritates you. Write down the person's name on your sheet. What are negative

aspects of that character? Write down three to five of their negative characteristics (over-confident, narcissistic, reactive, bossy, for example).

To help you with this exercise, I will share my responses:

1. I really admire Gandhi—he helped liberate India using a path of nonviolence. I admire his compassion, wisdom, and tenacity.
2. Donald Trump really gets under my skin! I hate his arrogance, narcissism, and that he likes being the focus of attention.

EXERCISE INSIGHTS

Here are insights you can gain when reviewing your responses to this exercise:

Question 1: We cannot recognize traits we do not ourselves possess at some level. I said I admired Gandhi for his compassion, so at some level, I also have the gift of compassion. Maybe it is not as developed as Gandhi's, but I have it and could develop it if I wanted. The good news is - you already possess many of the traits of the person you admire. Think of this person as your "Golden Mirror". They can represent a vision for how you could be if you develop your shared traits further.

Question 2: Here is the bad news, you may possess traits you judge in the person who irritates you. Probably, you avoid these traits or are blind to them. This negative person is a gift to you because they mirror the aspects of yourself you do not want to look at, and you can learn a lot about yourself by observing them and your reactions to their behaviors. You can think of them as your "Shadow Mirror", and they can be great teachers. I look at Trump and recognize that I, too, like to be the focus of attention. For instance, I wanted to write a chapter in this book. The good news is that as you recognize these traits in yourself, you can judge whether your approach to them makes sense.

OWNING YOUR SHADOW

Star Wars mythology introduced the concept of the dark side and the light side of the force. In Chinese philosophy, yin and yang describes how opposite or contrary forces may actually be complementary. Understanding both your strengths and "weaknesses" is essential for building self-awareness. *The shadow cannot exist without the light.*

Becoming aware of your negative or shadow traits can be uncomfortable. It can bring up shame or fear of judgement. Admitting to them, privately or to others, can be even more uncomfortable. Many of us cope with shame by burying it deep within us, avoiding shame as much as possible. We wear masks, projecting a view of ourselves that we think others will approve of and then wonder why our relationships feel empty. Earlier, I shared my story about how I learned about my relationship to anger and then how I learned to change my responses to anger. By sharing this story with you, I busted my own shame story. It is hard for someone to manipulate me when I am aware of my own shadow.

Without becoming conscious of these aspects of yourself, you will unconsciously react to triggering situations, becoming a victim to your own stories. By facing your stories and becoming self-aware, you start to understand yourself better. By owning your shadow aspects, you will be less controlled by them, and you start behaving from choice instead of purely reacting. You will recognize your limitations and take yourself out of situations for which your coping strategies are weak. You will know when to ask team members for help. As a project manager, the more authentically you own (all aspects of yourself), the more you enable your team to model the same. This is a key strategy for building trust, which is necessary for creating high-performing teams.

SUGGESTED NEXT STEPS

1. Reflect: pause and notice how you react to situations and specific people.
2. Journal: write about people in your life, including their positive and negative traits, and how you react to them—describe your emotions, how you feel strong or unsure of yourself in relation to them, and determine what you want to change.
3. Research: investigate self-awareness, emotional intelligence, and shadow work.
4. Support: look for support from counselors, self-help books, and other sources to identify your blind spots and to develop strategies that will address future challenges.
5. Talk: ask your team for feedback on your behaviors, and ask them to identify areas you could improve on.

BECOMING A SELF-AWARE PROJECT MANAGER

As a project manager, recognize that most people are unconscious of their shadow and that when experiencing change, they will behave in ways that seem irrational. By analyzing their reactions, you can help them develop strategies for navigating change.

Recognize your positive and negative reactions to other people, and determine how much of your reaction is conscious and unconscious. Recognize situations you avoid and decide how to manage them. For example, by recognizing your weak spots and triggers, you can admit you need help. You will have more compassion when you see how others also hide behind masks or act unconsciously.

I recommend exploring and developing your self-awareness. It may not be easy, but persevere and I promise you will become more confident, self-aware, and a much better project manager!

SOHAIL THAKER

Sohail is a Partner at Ethier, a Calgary, Alberta, Canada based management consulting firm. In a career spanning over three decades, Sohail has worked in North America, Africa, India, and Europe. Sohail's résumé includes project management (traditional, Agile), business analysis, business process innovation, organizational change management, and management consulting.

Ethier is a premier consulting firm that drives business excellence. For over 30 years, they have helped their clients realize their strategic goals with a focus on operational performance, risk and resilience, business transformation, and project delivery and resourcing. Their senior consultants bring a blend of experience, business acumen, and domain expertise to deliver business initiatives that consistently meet or exceed clients' expectations. Ethier works in collaboration with clients to adapt and prioritize efforts to meet business and project-specific needs and ensure a fit-for-purpose approach that delivers the desired benefits.

Sohail's accomplishments:

- MBA in International Business
- Certified Project Management Professional (PMP) with the Project Management Institute
- Prosci ADKAR certified

- Sohail in real life:
- Facilitates personal development workshops and counseling services
- Cosplayer, Star Trek geek, and Star Wars nerd, with dogs named Wookiee and Ewok
- Practices Iaido, the Japanese martial art of drawing the sword
- A born-again runner who ran the Calgary Marathon in 2014.

Sohail Thaker, MBA
E-mail: sthaker@ethier.ca
Website: www.ethier.ca
LinkedIn: Sohail Thaker

PEOPLE ARE THE KEY TO PROJECT SUCCESS
Do not forget the Stakeholder Analysis!

MICHELLE VENEZIA

Throughout the course of my career, I have had the opportunity to lead many different types of projects, across multiple industries:

- Implementation of a co-production facility at an off-shore customer location.
- Installation of a new, digital X-Ray platform at a veterinary clinic.
- Deployment of Office 365 across the enterprise.
- Start-up of a new project management office and introduction of Agile methodologies within an organization.

Although these initiatives were all very different, their ultimate success came down to one fundamental common factor – stakeholder buy-in and adoption.

In today's increasingly complex environment, no longer are projects created to deploy a new production version of a widget or push out a software patch. Projects often are the drivers of significant change in the user's or customer's daily behavior, workflow, or work environment. I have led very strong teams who thoroughly laid out the technical requirements of the projects. However, in most cases, I became the driver and sole voice asking the questions about day-to-day impact on the end user or customer.

As technology becomes more complex and tightly intertwined with all aspects of the business, the rate of change within organizations is higher than ever. Projects are often the vehicles for driving that change. McKinsey studies show that when excellent change management practices are included in a project, 94% of those projects meet or exceed stated objectives. Contrast that with poor change management, where only 15% of those projects met their stated objectives. The success of your project will ultimately be determined by the people impacted by its results – your stakeholders. The projects I have delivered that have yielded the most successful results were the ones where I took on the role as organizational change manager. My focus on the people related impacts of the project deliverables was the critical driver to my success.

WHO ARE YOUR STAKEHOLDERS?

When leading teams in delivering any change, the single most important tool you can leverage in all phases of your project is a stakeholder analysis. A strong stakeholder analysis, performed early during project initiation, is a powerful means to identify your stakeholders, understand what drives them, and develop an approach to engage them effectively.

The first step is to work with your team to identify your stakeholders. Consider the people engaged throughout your project, as well as those impacted by the outcome. This will include all of the traditional roles within your project (sponsor, project team, senior management), along with those impacted by the final project results. A simple post-it note brainstorming exercise with the team will help capture this critical list. Do not forget to capture the influencers within your organization whose buy-in on project deliverables may have the power to ultimately make or break the project outcome.

This step may seem intuitive, but failure to include the correct stakeholders upfront can have disastrous results. I recall an instance when working with an international customer, where we were sure we had all our bases covered when developing our project plan. Our direct customer was an in-country, co-production partner. We thought we understood all the key players on their team, and had developed close working relationships with most of them. We did a thorough stakeholder analysis throughout proposal development and built our project plan around the specific requirements of various members of this co-production partner's team. However, after over a year of significant investment in this proposal, we found out that our customer's customer, the end user, was not happy with our proposal. Our project plan centered on delivery of a state of the art in-country production facility for our direct customer, the co-production partner. However, the end user's primary consideration for contract award was delivery of a low-cost solution. We made proposal updates to address this key stakeholder's concerns, but it was too late and we ultimately lost the contract. It turned out that we had not considered the key factors that were important to that end user customer – we had barely addressed this end user in our project plan at all. Had we performed a thorough stakeholder identification we would have known to consider the particular needs of this end user client. Furthermore, our original proposal may have been more successful.

UNDERSTANDING YOUR STAKEHOLDERS

All stakeholders are not created equal. Therefore, once you have developed your stakeholder list, you will need to assess each stakeholder's influence level and level of interest in your project. A simple grid (*Figure 1*) works great – you can place the post-it notes directly into the quadrant that applies for each stakeholder. The quadrant where the stakeholder falls defines the expected level of effort that will be required on the part of your project team to engage that stakeholder throughout your project.

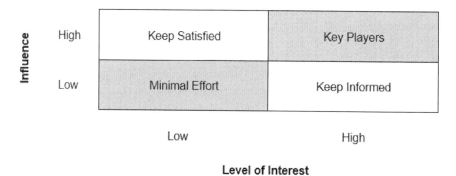

Figure 1: Stakeholder Influence/Interest Matrix

The results of this matrix are critical in development of your communications plan. Most often missed are those stakeholders that fall in the high influence/low interest category (keep satisfied). Although they may not be actively involved with your project, a negative perception of your plans or outcomes by these stakeholders has significant potential to derail your project team's efforts late in the game. The more strategic and highly visible your project is, the higher the likelihood of this happening.

If you are leading an agile transformation project, for example, you may focus on direct stakeholders and their senior leaders: the DevOps team, the PMO, the CIO (key players). It may not even occur to you to include the CFO and his/her staff in the ongoing stakeholder communications. However, if financial processes are not structured to support a model of continual assessment of benefits realization or incremental project funding, then the finance department may have the influence to stop your agile transformation in its tracks. Had you considered them as stakeholders in the "Keep Satisfied" quadrant, you could have anticipated their pain points early and provided regular updates throughout the project that addressed their concerns.

Based on where a stakeholder lies in the influence/interest grid, you can develop a more detailed analysis to support communications planning for each stakeholder group (*Figure 2*). The table shared here is a stakeholder analysis matrix in its simplest form. Your team may find it helpful to add columns to further define stakeholder information such as department name and stakeholder's role on the project.

Stakeholder Name	Engagement Level	Key Concerns
S1	Key Player	
S3	Key Player	
S2	Keep Informed	

Figure 2: Stakeholder Analysis Matrix

SIGNIFICANCE TO YOUR PROJECT

With a stakeholder analysis in place, you now have a foundation for development of a roadmap for your project. Stakeholders should be prioritized based on engagement level, with the most detailed planning needed for key players. You can begin building a communications plan that directly addresses each stakeholder's key concerns and keeps your stakeholders engaged at a frequency that is appropriate to their level. This one assessment will help you to address:

- Is your primary sponsor engaged at the appropriate level in the project?
- How well do your stakeholders understand their role in the success of your project?
- Can you leverage stakeholder groups to influence other stakeholders?
- What are the key concerns or trigger points that you need to address in your project planning?
- Are there potential project risks as a result of negative stakeholders?

You should reference and refresh this analysis throughout your project. You may consider dedicating a meeting to this effort prior to key project milestones. Stakeholders may change throughout the project, especially on large projects that span months or years. As the project progresses, you will also gain more visibility into the customer stakeholders and their requirements and concerns. This will help you to ensure you are not only delivering the right results, but also strengthen your plan for a superior project hand-off at completion. Even if you have successfully delivered all documented scope under budget and on time, if the results of your project are not adopted and maintained, your project may be considered a failure. A successful project close-out should include a last review of the stakeholder analysis to ensure all key concerns have been addressed. Do not make the mistake of many project teams of releasing wonderful technology, only to have it fall flat due to poor user adoption. Have you heard of Google Wave? Likely, not – although delivered as promised, user adoption was low and it was discontinued within a year because it never found a target audience.

Change is challenging, and the more change introduced by your project, the more risk your project will face. Save yourself and your team the potential of disaster that comes from forgetting the people side of project management! It is those people that will make or break your project. A stakeholder analysis matrix is a powerful tool for planning for those people, and keeping those plans forefront throughout your project.

MICHELLE VENEZIA

Michelle Venezia is the Director of the Project Portfolio Office at the University of Rochester Medical Center. She has a varied professional background spanning the healthcare, IT technology, medical device, and defense industries. She has led the successful start-up of several PMOs, and has led global teams in the US, Europe, and Asia. She is also an adjunct faculty member in Brandeis University's Graduate Professional Studies program, and the Owner of NicAri Strategic Services, a professional provider of Project, Program, and Portfolio Management training and consulting services.

Michelle holds a B.S. degree in Industrial Engineering from SUNY Buffalo, an MBA from Penn State University, and Portfolio Management Professional, Project Management Professional, and Agile Certified Practitioner certifications from the Project Management Institute (PMI). She is also a Prosci Certified Change Management Practitioner and Certified ScrumMaster. She has held various board level roles with the PMI Rochester Chapter including Chapter President. Michelle is a 2019 graduate of PMI's Leadership Institute Master Class (LIMC).

Michelle Venezia, PfMP, PMP, ACP
University of Rochester Medical Center
NicAri Strategic Services, LLC
Rochester, NY
https://www.linkedin.com/in/mlvenezia/

michelle.venezia@nicariservices.com

585-369-6220

LOST AND FOUND

CONNIE WYATT

LOST AND FOUND

There is something lost on many projects that is difficult to identify. As project managers, we know something is missing, but we cannot quite put our finger on it. Project tasks and activities are being accomplished, but are we truly executing what is essential to complete the scope of the project based on the needs of the business and the management plan? Perhaps the scope has spiraled out of control, and we are trying to determine what happened? In most cases, we can trace it back to missing requirements. But when requirements are not tracked adequately, how do we find that which is lost? Requirements traceability is the answer! This "best" practice is often lost in the shuffle of managing other responsibilities that are more widely known and respected as "good" project management. When we, as project managers, execute on the best practice of consistent requirements management, it improves our ability to manage effectively and prevent the scope from veering off track. At times, we toss aside requirements by management as being the business analyst's job. Instead, our goal should be ensuring requirements traceability occur, as opposed to being traditional thinkers in terms of who manages the process.

HOW TO START THE JOURNEY RIGHT

When thinking about requirements traceability, identifying a good tool or template to ensure you have captured the client's needs is vital. There are many software applications and a seemingly countless number of templates in the marketplace! Finding which works best for your project and the user is where the journey begins. An example of a simple tool that I find particularly useful is seen in below (Exhibit A).

Exhibit A - Requirements Template

Requirement Description	Requirement Type	Priority	Responsible Area/ Department/ Individual	Date Captured	PI or Fix Note	Fix Notes/ Recommendation	Gap Analysis/ Assessment/ Solution Recommendation	Resource Responsible	Estimated Effort (Hours/Cost)	Status	Accepted/ Rejected Date	Accepted/ Rejected By
	Business	1-High				Yes					Accepted	
	Solution	2-Medium									Rejected	
	Functional	3-Low										
	Nonfunctional											
	Stakeholder											
	Technical											
	Transition											

This tool can utilized by any resource person assigned to your project – business analyst, project coordinator, or you – the project manager! If the project has limited resources, you can and should take on this responsibility. Do not get bogged down thinking about what "should" happen or who "should" take the lead. As project managers and effective leaders, we should be less focused on which team member might traditionally address each responsibility, and more focused on the benefits gained by tracking the completion of each requirement that subsequently leads to the successful conclusion of the project. There are always team dynamics that require the project manager to lead with patience and grace. However, it is important to ensure that everyone is aware of your willingness to support the team and help accomplish all tasks, even those that go beyond what might be considered "typical" for a project manager.

Key elements to include in a tracking system may vary depending upon what other systems or applications are being used for scope management. In general, my experience has shown that project managers need to think about these standard criteria in the requirements traceability process:

- Requirement Description
- Requirement Type (Business, functional, technical, and so on)
- Priority
- Requesting Area / Department / Individual
- Date Captured
- Fit or Gap
- Fit – Solution Recommendation
- Gap – Analysis Assessment / Solution Recommendation
- Resource Responsible (for requirement completion)
- Estimated Effort (time or cost)
- Status – Accepted / Rejected / Deferred
- Accepted / Rejected Date
- Accepted / Rejected By (Individual's Name)

In reviewing Exhibit A, this simple spreadsheet provides one approach and outlines the type of requirements traceability criteria that lead to successful scope completion. When considering how to keep a project on track, start with choosing a method to manage what you are tracking. In an Agile or iterative project approach, you may document your requirements in the form of a user story on a product backlog. That is fine. The method may vary, but the more important point is that you get it done and it is in a usable format for traceability through testing. Having a solid solution (whether it be software or a template) that provides you with a way to map your requirements journey will keep them from being lost. It is also important to obtain signoff from your project sponsor as well as document revision history for scope changes post signoff to manage the process.

So why do not project managers trace requirements? In most cases, it is time. To support the scope, we usually find the time to document project requirements, but struggle with time management and implementing an approach that will track each element for the duration of the project. Also, planning for requirements elicitation is different for every project. How much time do you need to gather them all? How many stakeholders do you need to talk to? What is your approval process to ensure that the project's critical success factors are met in the end? Without a process, we are left wondering where the requirements got lost. It is easy to pin-point how this happened when you examine more deeply.

WHAT HAPPENS WHEN THERE IS NO JOURNEY MAP

I once managed a project where I was asked to join the team as the project manager in the middle of the implementation. The scope was broad and the existing project manager was wearing too many hats serving in other roles to really be successful in managing the overall engagement. Initially, it was a struggle. All of the team members were very technical and great application developers, but no one had written down a single thing: No requirements. No design document. Nothing! They just talked to stakeholders, determined what they wanted, and built it. That strategy sounds great until you are in a position of trying to gain clarity about requests, the original requirement, or what was in or out of scope.

The scope changed every day! No one could really confirm if we were close to meeting the stakeholders' needs or remotely in a position of being on time or budget. Were there any gaps? Are we giving the client what was requested? The dilemma was readily apparent. It was an uphill climb and we had to take a few steps backward to make some giant leaps forward to get the project done. The process started by going back to the basics, which involved going back to the beginning to connect with key stakeholders to elicit their requirements, objectives, and critical success factors for the project. Following that process, we combined all of this information into a comprehensive requirements traceability solution to understand what we had (or had not) already accomplished, and where we needed to go to get the project back on track.

If you lack project documentation on the front end, in the end, it is almost guaranteed to be confounding trying to determine what is actually in scope and if all requirements have been fulfilled. As project managers, we have to take the lead in making sure this deliverable is satisfied as a means of achieving true client satisfaction by delivering on the overall objectives and scope.

WE HAVE MISSING REQUIREMENTS; BUT, I HAD AN APPROACH. WHAT WENT WRONG?

On the best project, a project manager can still have execution problems. Having a requirements traceability approach is good; using it is better. Whether following a waterfall, Agile, or iterative project methodology, it is imperative that you include time in your plan to actually execute on your traceability approach. Knowing that you have documented everything for your journey, makes you confident that your project is starting off correctly, but you must ensure that you create a cadence to complete the process.

Taking the time to plan your strategy makes sense. Things get off track when you have not created an approach that is reasonable to follow while executing the project. To prevent this from occurring, we have to think about what we can actually achieve and then ensure that we put the time and a plan in place to make it happen. When you leave the traceability process on the side of the road, the journey to a successfully implemented project will be long and arduous.

CONCLUSION

As a project manager, you want to be known for completing projects on time and on budget, but also for helping your stakeholders meet their needs. To sum up how important requirements are to a client - even when you think you have done your best, they still want to know they got what they requested.

Satisfying requirements and having a clear understanding of any gaps that may exist is the best way to ensure that the organization's objectives are met. When operating as effectively and efficiently as possible, the requirements traceability process can be successful. The client's needs were met to their specifications, and as the project manager, you can feel confident that the scope was accomplished. Upon completion of your project, you can rest assured that no requirements are left waiting at the Lost and Found!

CONNIE WYATT

As President and CEO of S.A.I.D. Strategy Group, Incorporated, Connie Wyatt has been helping teams reach their goals in project management, business process design, and business analysis for over 20 years. A certified PMP® and PMI-PBA®, she has led projects focusing on strategic business initiatives, hardware/server deployments, software application development, and business process design. Connie and the team at S.A.I.D. Strategy have provided their management consulting expertise on engagements within the philanthropy, higher education, and financial services industries along with supporting small businesses looking for improved efficiency in their operations. As a project problem solver, she has the ability to build collaborative working relationships with clients to drive projects forward. Her communications expertise extends to include senior leadership, executive sponsor, and stakeholder communications addressing organizational change to achieve strategic business initiatives. Connie has assisted organizations in project management office implementations to create systems that work within organizations' culture for successful portfolio management including reviews of project performance and metrics.

Connie F. Wyatt, PMP®, PMI-PBA®
President
S.A.I.D. Strategy Group, Inc.
connie@saidstrategy.com

847-660-7751
www.saidstrategy.com
linkedin: conniewyatt

Kathi Soniat can be reached at ksoniat77@gmail.com

David Barrett can be reached at dbarrett@solutionsnetwork.com

The Keys to Our Success – first edition is available on Amazon

Made in the USA
Middletown, DE
30 September 2020